Before You Were Born

Authored by

MARGUERITE ROCHOLL

ISBN: 1478220392
ISBN 13: 9781478220398

WITH LOVE TO

REGINA
JACQUELINE
CHRISTIAN
THREE EXTRAODNARY EVENTS IN MY LIFE
&
TED
WHO MADE IT ALL POSSIBLE

Chapter

1

These are the memories of a very ordinary childhood. You might think that my thoughts would not be worthy of such a lengthy read but sometimes even an ordinary life can have some extraordinary days. I am hopeful that when this journey is completed, you will know me in a novel way, not just as your mother but as a middle child, an obedient daughter, the blond sister, and finally the obedient blonder middle child who rushed hell-bent into that dreaded, scary zone-the teenager. There are times when I seem to be a spectator of my own life and perhaps that is another reason I began this wordy effort: to finally put to sleep all the childhood memories that enter uninvited into my everyday musings and become entwined in so many of my thoughts and words. And lastly, and perhaps the most important, it is an opportunity for you to come to know the interesting lives of your grandparents and our colorful Irish background.

Ushering the past to meet the present has helped me to appreciate two wonderful human beings, my parents, Marguerite and Bud. I have come to know them as two individuals who were very much in love, with a full life that was, much to my surprise, totally separate from being my parents. I enjoyed the pursuit that followed the lives of a young couple who were part of what would later be called the "Greatest Generation." They met during Prohibition, married during the Depression, and were patriotic citizens who supported the war effort during World War II. They had the strong work ethic of their generation while sharing the deep faith of their parents. Their life had much joy and occasional sorrow, with lean years and better years, but through it all, there was an abundance of love and, most important, much laughter.

They married in 1933 during the Great Depression. It was a desperate economic time that affected the entire country, with over one million workers out of work. My parents, however, were among the fortunate to be employed. Bud went to work as a longshoreman on the New York docks after his high school graduation and my mother, Marguerite was employed as a clerk in the office of a large discount department chain. Although they each brought home a weekly pay check, their future remained very uncertain.

Banks failed and the stock market crashed, leaving families across the nation with little hope, very hungry and so very desperate. Some of the wealthiest, who considered themselves with the most to lose, chose suicide from the buildings that were once home to their success. The newlyweds were able to pay their rent and purchase the necessities but the threat of their personal financial collapse was always just a payday away.

Over the years, when the subject of managing finances came up, my mother would remind us that they were the victims of the Great Depression. There were those who struggled through the depression that would never again spend money frivolously. They would continue to live a very frugal life, always expecting the past to become the present. My parents, however, were not included in this cautious group. Carpe diem! They lived for the moment, seized the day, and along the way occasionally spent more than they should.

A favorite book of mine is *David Copperfield* by Charles Dickens.

I read it as a young teenager and, in spite of my adolescent perception, I was quick to recognize my parents when I met the

Micawbers. They were typical Dickens's characters: eccentric, real, and interesting. The Micawbers, a loyal and loving couple, had many creditors and very little credit.

They would worry and fret about the future but, when or if a small amount of cash came into their lives, they celebrated with their entire windfall. A quote from this classic that best describes Mrs. Micawber's ability to cope with their dire financial straits reads as follows: "Mrs. Micawber was very elastic. I have known her to be thrown into fainting fits by the King's taxes at three o'clock and eat lamb chops, and drink warm ale at four o'clock."

My parents shared some similarities with the Micawbers; both couples worried about their finances while enjoying the good life and sought refuge from their worries with their evening libation.

Chapter

2

On Sunday afternoons, my mother would sit at her desk, diligently writing checks as drops of sweat trickled down her forehead. She was attempting to balance the family checkbook. There was an aura that surrounded her that, even at an early age, we recognized as stress and instinctively we knew to be quiet and keep ourselves busy.

You remember Grandma's desk; it was her personal power point. The desk, a tall, narrow, attractive piece of furniture, is referred to as a secretary. It consisted of three separate sections. The top section — a book case — boasted two decorative glass doors that protected Grandma's precious possessions, her collection of poetry, and a few classic novels. Her favorites were those inscribed by Bud with his love to his beautiful Marge and these pages are worn from repetitive use.

My mother had a passion for books and every week she would take her two preschoolers on the bus to visit the Rockaway Library. Rosanne and I would return home feeling as smug as the fisherman who made a great catch. We would find a cozy corner and curl up with a kitten and our new favorite book. Although we did not know how to read, it really did not matter; we would enjoy the pictures and create our own story.

I am sure there were days when our mother read to us but I don't remember it being a part of our daily routine. One summer morning she did read a poem to us. It was very sad and it became a lasting childhood memory.

LITTLE BOY BLUE

The little toy dog is covered with dust
But sturdy and staunch he stands;
And the little toy soldier is red with rust
And his musket moulds in his hands,
Time was when the little toy dog was new,
And the soldier was passing fair,
And that was the time when our little boy blue
Kissed them and put them there.
"Now don't you go till I come," he said
"And don't you make any noise!"
So toddling off to his trundle bed
He dreamt of his pretty toys.
And as he was dreaming, an angel song
Awakened our Little Boy Blue,
Oh, the years are many, the years are long
But the little toy friends are true!
Ay, faithful to Little Boy Blue they stand,
Each in the same old place.
Awaiting the touch of a little hand
The smile of a little face,
And they wonder, as waiting these long years
Through,
In the dust of the little chair,
What has become of our Little Boy Blue
Since he kissed them and put them there.

EUGENE FIELD 1850–1895

Most of my early memories are frozen images that come to me in single frames, occasionally with a voice that connects me to my past. A vivid image is a memory of that summer day when my mother removed a small book from the shelf and began to recite a poem that traumatized two little girls.

It might have been her favorite poem; over the years it had touched the lives of so many and was subsequently put to music that lulled children to sleep. I could not accept that the angels took this little boy from his parents, so I focused my sadness on his loyal toys patiently waiting for their friend who would never return.

Chapter

3

It seems to me that some sixty years ago, it never occurred to parents that perhaps some children's books, poems, or movies might contribute to occasional nightmares or chronic sleepwalking. These venues, which were almost all of our entertainment, introduced us to some explicit, gruesome murder and mayhem, hate, and evil.

I was quite an accomplished sleepwalker, actually very good at it. On any given night I could be found wandering around the house while the rest of the family was fast asleep. On one particular night, with a full moon high tide, I was on my way out the back door when my mother found me and led me back to bed. If she hadn't found me, it could have been an interesting walk. Our backyard had no fence to separate a sleepwalker from the ten-foot span of yard and the six-foot depth of salt water.

When I was finally six years old, my birthday gift from my brother Michael was a trip to the movies to see *Bambi*. I was very excited that cold January afternoon when we left our house to walk to the bus stop. The bus was usually late but I could not take my eyes off the boulevard, praying silently that it had not already passed our corner.

Living up to its reputation, it was predictably late but finally the old green bus pulled up and the door opened. With great excitement and help from my brother, I climbed the steps and boarded my coach. As Michael deposited our fare in the box, I changed my seat several times, finally settling for a window seat behind the driver, thinking he might just want to chat.

My face was pressed against the window as the driver pulled out and I watched the familiar streets of my town pass by. The window was foggy from my breath and I wiped it with the sleeve of my coat just in time to see my grandparents' car returning from Sunday Mass.

We passed a few houses that still wore their Christmas decorations.It reminded me that my mother insisted our decorations be taken down by January 6, Little Christmas. She was always a bit set in her ways when it came to the holidays.

A once beautiful Christmas tree lays discarded and abandoned by the curb, tossed out by the very family who, just a few weeks ago, were thrilled to bring it home and decorate it as a symbol of their family Christmas. The only evidence of its previous stature were the few strands of silver tinsel. It wouldn't be long before some local boys would drag it out onto the frozen bay and set it afire.

We stopped at a traffic light and, looking down the street, I could see my new friend's house. We both had a part in the first-grade Christmas nativity play; he was a shepherd and I was an angel. His father's small boat, covered with canvas, sat frozen in their yard, where it would remain for the winter. I thought it would make a great hiding place when he played hide and seek with his friends.

The old bus shifted gears and we progressed down the boulevard, passing the elegant old carousel and the deserted grounds of the summer day camp until we finally approached the draw bridge and stopped at the toll booth. I didn't know what it cost for this large bus but my father paid ten cents for our car the day before when we crossed the bay.

My mother laughed one day when she told me that when I was very little, I was afraid to drive over a bridge. I told her I did not want to get my new shoes wet. My anxieties obviously began very early but this bridge was a familiar friend.

The old draw bridge was the umbilical cord for Broad Channel. It offered a broader life than we knew on the island; most important to us children were the wide, sandy beaches. My memory frequently replays the hot summer days that Rosanne and I spent at the ocean beach. Filling our pails with shells, we walked the beach laughing as we chased our footprints when the foamy surf washed them away. The Rockaways also provided the necessities: a hospital, doctors and dentist, a high school, and a variety of shops and stores not to be found in our small town.

We were driving a little faster then and when we reached the top of the bridge, I was looking down at a red tug boat pushing large chunks of ice aside as it towed a barge through the dark blue water topped with a dusting of white caps. I knew that soon we would be arriving at the 116th Street Park Theater.

The cold air was cruel and the wind blustery as we stepped down from the bus; we were just a few feet from the reach of the restless Atlantic Ocean. Michael walked faster than I, but we were both anxious to escape the cold, so I struggled to keep up with him. As we approached the window to purchase our tickets, we both noticed the large graphic promotional posters of the current feature and there was not a hint of *Bambi* to be found among them.

Michael appeared nervous and stressed; he knew he was facing a complicated decision. Should he take a six-year-old to see a movie entitled *Our Four-Poster Bed*, or should we stand in the cold for two long hours and wait for the return bus?

He bought the tickets and we sat through what was for me a very boring movie. It was not, however, very boring when we returned home a few hours later. My mother turned a very odd shade of gray as her jaw dropped when I described the movie that we had just seen.

A few weeks later, my mother researched the movie schedule, this time with success. She found a theater that was actually showing *Bambi* and Michael and I headed out again.

I was enjoying this beautiful animated film but was not prepared for what was coming next…and then it happened. Bambi's mom was shot by a man with a gun. The theater was filled to capacity with small children, who sat with tears streaming down their faces. We were watching our worst nightmare, the death of a young mother and an orphan left alone to fend for himself. Bambi represented to every one of us sitting there the unthinkable, our own mother dying.

The fairy tales of my youth were not new. Many generations before us were subjected to the same gruesome tales. It was not unusual to read a child a bedtime story that included the wolf that ate the heroine's grandmother. The reader is relieved at the "happy" ending when the woodsman, with a sharp ax, kills the wolf and saves Red Riding Hood.

My favorite Disney movie is *Ashputtel*, more commonly known as *Cinderella*. This fairy tale tells the story of a lovely but abused orphaned girl who was bullied by her stepmother and two ugly stepsisters. The ending was predictably happy, with Cinderella marrying Prince Charming, but there is a message: beautiful people are good and will live happy lives; the homely are bad and stepmothers are mean and not to be trusted.

I did enjoy *Snow Drop*, aka *Snow White*. Here we have a little girl who is condemned to death by her mother, the queen, because she is just too beautiful. She finds refuge with new friends, seven male dwarfs. She spends her days cooking, cleaning, and doing the dwarves' laundry when they are off to work. She is ultimately poisoned by the queen but Snow White is saved by the kiss of a handsome prince, who will soon become her husband.

Perhaps good conquering evil was the intended subliminal message but I would certainly not choose *Hansel and Gretel* as a bedtime story for any child.

On a winter afternoon, too windy and cold to play outside, my mother would pull out the seventy-eight vinyl records. Rosanne and I would climb up on the couch, a few kittens on our lap, ready to hear some of our favorite fairy tales and the one I remember best was a tale about strange talking fish.

Children were boating out on deep water when they suddenly fell over the side of the boat and into the sea. This story did not upset me; I loved the water, so I was okay with it. The children explored a new world on the bottom of the ocean and discovering the city of Atlantis.

After I sat through of a few fairy tales, my nervous stomach was letting me know what would be next. I tried to be nonchalant and perfectly calm when *Hansel and Gretel* began. The only clue of my apprehension was the intensity with which I stroked my kitten. The fur on her back appeared to be getting somewhat sparse. This was not the first time I had sat through this story and I knew what was coming next.

Two siblings, a boy and a girl, are sent into the woods by their wicked father to look for berries. The innocent little brother and sister do not know that their father's plan is to abandon them when they lost their way. He was at home building two little coffins.

It is getting dark when they realize they are hopelessly lost and begin to look for a place to spend the night. They foolishly enter the witch's sugary cottage.

I found excuses to leave the room: I am thirsty. Is it raining? I think I need the bathroom. The kitten needs a bathroom. I could bear it no longer. I covered my ears and left the room. My mother would find me later under the bed, protected from the finale of this disturbing tale. I knew the traumatizing finale and I did not want to hear it again. The witch tries to put Gretel in the oven but Gretel is clever and outsmarts her. She pushes the witch into the hot oven, leaving her to die a painful and miserable death, to the joy of everyone.

In spite of my occasional sleepwalking associated with the grim Grimm's tales, I inherited my mother's love for books. My fondest childhood memories usually include a book. A special birthday gift was a book by Dorothy Canfield called *Understood Betsy*. It was my first hard cover book and I would have trouble putting it down especially when it was time to do my homework. I enjoyed meeting Elizabeth and exploring her simple but lovely life.

On Christmas morning, when the elf dust had settled, I would curl up on the couch with a favorite Christmas gift, a new book. The Christmas tree which had dominated our living room was now surrounded by a surplus of gifts that Santa had left the night before. In the background, Theresa Brewer was singing her favorites from a new LP record, a gift to my father.

It was a perfect Christmas moment. I would relieve my red stocking, which hung precariously from the mantel of our cardboard fireplace, of a few chunks of chocolate and then open to the latest escapades of my two favorite characters.

I left home for a time and followed a new adventure of Cherry Ames, a very perky nurse with soft black curls, or Nancy Drew, an amazing sleuth for her young age. I have lost touch with Nancy and Cherry but I never lost my love for books and chocolate.

Chapter

4

Your Grandma's secretary stood tall alongside her throne, her very own white high-back chair, where she presided over her family. When the desktop was down, it made a convenient table for her Manhattan, her book and reading glasses, or her exhausted rosary. A special treat for her grandchildren was to sit at the desk, fortified with crayons and paper to create some "Grandma artwork." Some serious work was produced but they all knew not to disturb Grandma's "important papers."

This also was a center of stress during her bookkeeping sessions.

After one of these sessions, Grandma and Bud would have a serious financial discussion, each nodding in complete agreement that they must and would change their spending habits. It had all the intentions of the inception of a new trendy diet and would last just as long.

A few days following their chat, my mother was on the train to Brooklyn, stopping at Hoyt and Schmerhorn, home to her favorite department store, Abraham and Strauss, for a bit of necessary shopping. I was a bit perplexed; I had just been a witness to their agreement of frugality.

On one occasion, the ground rent was due and she was worried how they would manage to meet the payment. I am sure her evening prayers included a request to St. Jude, her favorite saint. It might have been the intercession of St. Jude or simply fate but they were invited to Roosevelt Racetrack as the guest of the management. They looked forward to the night out and possibly their introduction to horse racing. Placing a bet on the first two races, they chose our house numbers, five and five, for a daily double. It might have been beginners' luck but in both races their horse came in and they went home with the ground rent and a thank you to St. Jude.

In their defense, our bills were always paid on time and they were very generous to charities. Leaving her house one day when she was about eighty years old and living alone, I picked up her stamped mail and offered to drop it in the mailbox. As I was checking each envelope for postage, I noticed all eight were checks to separate charities.

They loved each other, loved their children, and loved a good time. They weren't perfect but they gave us a very happy and secure childhood.

Chapter

5

There are times when I hear interesting news or bits of gossip and my first instinct is to share it with my mother. I am about to reach for the phone and then of course I realize she won't be answering. She hasn't answered for fifteen years. And there are also times when I find myself talking silently to my mom.; I tell her how I understand…I finally get it.

Grandma Marguerite outlived Bud by twelve years. We were committed from the day he died to take care of her, keep her busy, and try to make her happy, if even just a little.

I did not expect it to be easy; we all had busy lives but we learned to juggle our schedules to adjust to Grandma's new life. As determined as we were, I had some trepidation looking toward the future. I wanted to protect Grandma and let her know she was needed but I also wanted to be able to look forward to a new freedom that comes with the empty nest.

As aware as I was of Grandma's grief, I doubt that I could ever empathize with the depth of her pain. She would always keep a brave front and offer a quick smile. She appeared happy but I know now that she was always tormented by her loss of

Bud, the love of her life. For the fifty-three years of their marriage, Grandma's life was Bud.

Grandma Marguerite was a stay-at-home mom, as were most of the mothers in Broad Channel. Some eighty years ago, it would be rare for a mother to work outside her home. Two parents, each with their individual role—that's just the way it was and I was happy with that.

There was a popular Jack Jones song in the '60s and the lyrics offered advice for women in love and how to keep your man from straying; they went something like this, "Comb your hair, fix your makeup, time to get ready for love." The message, not very subtle, was that there would always be someone at the office, prettier and ready to take your man.

I remember at the time thinking how sexist this sounded, but Grandma would not have it any other way. She would stop her housework at around 4:00 PM and before she started dinner, she showered and dressed up, complete with makeup and perfume, anticipating Bud's return home. Sitting in her white chair, she would begin her rosary. Twenty years later, feminists would call this slavery; Grandma would call it a privilege.

Sometime around six-thirty, he would drive down Fifteenth Road, blowing the car horn, letting Marguerite and everyone else in a two-block radius know that he was home. A seven thirty dinner was late for me and Rosanne, so we would have our dinner and be ready for bed before he came home. This was their time, her special time of day.

We knew that we were an important part of their life but we also knew that they were first to each other. They would toast each other with a chilled Manhattan, followed by dinner with animated conversation about their day but mostly it was about him. He spoke of his work and the news event that he had covered that day, always wondering if his photograph would be on the front page of tomorrow's *Daily News*. His Marge was very supportive of his career, a good listener, and she made the perfect Manhattan.

If she was our burden after Bud died, it was only to keep her happy and her days interesting. This was a difficult challenge; they had a lifetime of amazing adventures during their life together and it would never be possible for us to keep her days as interesting as they had been with Bud. Her phone would ring several times a day; we each had our own convenient time to call. Her home would always be the epicenter of our family, with her receiving at least one visitor each day from one of the family members. A primary concern for all was that she continued to live there as long as she wanted.

We kept her calendar booked with celebrations of birthdays, graduations, anniversaries, and weddings. As the family grew, so did her social life. If it was a quiet week, she was invited to one of our homes for a simple home-cooked dinner accompanied by a glass of her favorite wine.

These family celebrations gave her days to look forward to. She would take the time to choose the perfect outfit for every occasion. She continued to love fashion and never ceased to be a glamorous lady, dressing age-appropriate with elegance and style. We would return the favor by complimenting her and letting her know how pretty she looked. I loved to see her dress up, hats and coats perfectly coordinated and her dress with the right accessories. It was her gift to us. I knew that everything was okay when she cared about her appearance.

She had a genius for remembering every birthday and wedding anniversary. She was sad if we were sad and delighted for us when we were happy.

Mother's Day was a family affair that began with Mass and was followed by an eclectic brunch at Grandma's, everyone bringing a favorite food and bearing gifts. She would receive an assortment of flowers, hanging baskets, cut flowers, and potted plants. A large bouquet of lilacs, a gift from Bud, had arrived every year on Mother's Day, his thank you to his Marge for his four children. I was anxious not to have the empty vase facing her in the morning. A generous stranger solved that when she gave me beautiful lilacs from her garden for my mother.

She spent the day surrounded by a family who love her. After, the dishes were cleaned and the folding chairs put away, it was time to gather up the kids and head for home. Leftovers were wrapped and goodbyes were said and she was alone once more. She did not mind; she was tired but it was a good tired.

She would always love a day shopping with her girls: her daughters and granddaughters. We all loved the challenge of the hunt, finding the perfect treasure, and, only after being approved by all, bringing it home.

The special memory of one day of shopping will always bring a smile to my face. Grandma Marguerite and the three sisters went to the Brooklyn A&S to shop for baby gifts. We took the subway and, when we stopped to buy our tokens, the clerk in the booth took a long, hard stare at us. She was rather startled but in her defense we did look a bit odd. The three sisters were all in their final trimester of pregnancy.

My mom winked at the clerk and told her, "Don't worry, it is not contagious." Never one to be shy, I added, "We are actually members of the Irish Catholic Propagation Society." Mary began first, as we descended the stairs to the platform, her great contagious laugh. Rosanne followed with her loud, rock-the-room howl of laughter. I suspect that a few of the commuters on the platform thought she was in the late stages of labor.

Chapter

6

The first Christmas after Bud died was surely our most difficult holiday. We would always do our best to help our mother celebrate Christmas without changing the way it had always been. We carried on as though everything were the same but there was a great sadness, very visible by the empty place at the head of the table. The birth of Grandma's second great-grandchild, Raquel, on Christmas day was a wonderful diversion from our melancholy and we were grateful for a reason to be happy. A new life came into the family the same year he left us.

A group effort kept her holiday merry for the years that followed. Mary's sons would buy the tree and place it in her living room the same way Bud had for so many years. Mary and I would bring down the Christmas decorations from the attic and, under her strict supervision, we began our chore of sorting through the many boxes that held a lifetime of precious memories.

Pavarotti serenaded us with beautiful holiday music as we created another Christmas throughout her home. We snacked on Grandma's banana bran muffins, complemented with a warm drink, as we completed the festive mission. A day of Christmas shopping and lunch was planned with more emphasis on the lunch than the shopping. This was family at its best.

I have many joyful Christmas memories and also some that are very sad. It is a time to reflect on the past and the many friends and family members who left us forever during previous holiday seasons. All these memories blend together but the sad ones seem to rise to the top.

I am in a department store that is beautifully decorated and I hear a favorite but sentimental Christmas song playing throughout the store. I suddenly feel very sad and I wipe my eyes to conceal the tears that expose my vulnerability. Music that was written and sang to inspire joy at times for me is reflective and emotional. Like the ghost of Christmas past, who visits Scrooge on Christmas Eve, the spirits of loved ones, all too young to die, surround me in the days before Christmas.

December is a poignant month. It is the end of another year, never to be seen again, with mistakes made that cannot be undone. We say goodbye to a time of our life that has now become a memory and has produced both some blissful and melancholy moments.

On Christmas Eve, the family attends a late afternoon Mass and we return to her home for our annual tree trimming. It is another moment of mixed emotions, entering the house that defined my childhood; our family is no longer the same. Your Grandma, removing her coat, comments how she loves the St. Luke's Christmas gospel and we all agree that we enjoyed the innocent music of the children's choir. She seems quiet and pensive.

Her children, son-in-laws, grandchildren, grandchildren's boyfriends, girlfriends, and great-grandchildren—the numbers grow every year—were all together to celebrate with her.

The scent of the Balsam fir is a sweet and familiar perfume that filters through each room with a whisper of pine and we recognize that it is now finally Christmas. If we were the last to arrive, we greet and are greeted by thirty-something members of the family. Everyone who is of age, and a few who are not, are sipping champagne with hor d' oeuvres.

24

There is a merry Christmas kiss and hug for everyone while commenting that this tree surely is the best we have ever seen. Grandma has changed into a dark green velvet hostess gown and is pleased with the "oohs" and "ahs" of her admirers. She holds her favorite stem glass, half filled with wine, and raises it to toast her family.

The house, warm and cozy, is immune to the cold winter afternoon; the winter solstice has begun. The clock chimes five and the sun begins to set on another Christmas Eve. The brilliant red globe rests on the horizon, preparing to wake up the part of the world that Santa has already visited. There are folks sitting here on far-away beaches waiting for a first sign of the miracle we call sunrise. But at this moment the sun is so close, I imagine I can reach out and touch it. The bay has frozen over and the blazing red of the setting sun reflects on the smooth ice, turning it to deep shades of pink and blue. A solitary seagull hovers over the bay, searching for a break in the ice and his Christmas meal. This is the vista from Grandma's living room. It is our favorite time of day.

This was his moment. Bud's personal Christmas tradition was repeated each year when he gathered the family around him to share in the sunset. He would point out that the sun is setting exactly between the towers of the Marine Parkway Bridge as it does at this exact time every Christmas Eve. We would raise our glass, toasting each other and creating a new Christmas moment.

Now it is time for a final decorating task. We will transform a lovely but naked tree into our beautiful Christmas vision. It is almost dark; Grandma Marguerite will sit in her tall white chair in a very crowded living room, directing the grandchildren where to place the ornaments. Her special antique favorites, bought for their first Christmas, are designated to a tall and trusted adult. When it is finally completed, a hush descends over the room. As the overhead lights are dimmed, someone assumes Bud's traditional role and turns the switch which lights our tree to the applause of the family who are wishing he was still here.

Coffee is served and we sit back and sense that the Christmas Eve magic is upon us. We exhale and realize the shopping is over; tonight we have experienced the peace and joy of the Christmas

Mass, knowing that this night is going to be a difficult night for children to fall asleep but, above all, how fortunate we are.

We say our goodnights and leave her alone to spend her first Christmas morning in an empty house. We placed small gifts under the tree, giving her something to open as she waits for the phone to ring on Christmas day. It does not take long before the calls begin—family and friends wishing her a merry Christmas and making sure she is okay.

The Rocholls are at home on Christmas morning, if for just a few short hours. We gather around our beautiful Christmas tree of green plastic manufactured in China, but we are very happy with our lovely fireproof Christmas tree. The faux fir is trimmed with ornaments that commemorate the times and travel of our family's lives.

We have almost completed our exchange of gifts when it crosses my mind that probably right at this moment, every child in our neighborhood is opening identical toys and clothes. It is the same every year, the have-to-have list that sends parents on a maddening treasure hunt, lining up at toy stores at 6:00 AM. Our family has grown and now there are different toys, considerably more expensive, but the toys and clothes still remain almost identical to their friends'. Muffin loves her rubber toy and is wearing several plastic bows on her oval head. Poor thing, at one time she was a cute puppy.

The apprehension is almost over. There is always one or two gifts that give me trouble sleeping on Christmas Eve. There is so much anticipation; I see myself handing over that one wrapped gift that I thought was not affordable yet somehow managed to bring home. I am sure that I outdid myself this year.

Not all gifts are as appreciated by the receiver as they are by the donor. There is an unwritten code, however: you must love the gift for at least a few hours and then it is a very delicate communication to convey your honest opinion to the giver. A misplaced comma or a slight inflection on any syllable might result in the dreaded words: "You don't like it; you have ruined my Christmas." This year, however, was a success.

We clear the house of wrapping paper, gently remove the glued bows from the dog—even three bows won't make this dog pretty—and then we dress for Christmas day. The car is packed with food and wrapped gifts as we five head over the North Channel Bridge and through the snow to Grandma's house.

It is standing room only when we arrive at her house bearing gifts and food. It is a wonderful chaos, exchanging gifts and feeding twenty-something people in a room designed for ten. Grace is said and we share another Christmas dinner but we omit our annual prayer, thanking God that once again we are all together.

Before the Christmas season comes to a close, Dad and I take Grandma to visit Bud's grave. There are small stones on his headstone, which let us know that he had a recent visitor.

It is always a cold and windy day when we take the long ride out to the cemetery on Long Island. We push the snow away from his grave and then each take Grandma by the arm and carefully walk her to his place. We say a short, silent prayer and meditate about his life,that was interrupted too soon.

I never look forward to the visit; sometimes I even dread it. December is always such a very busy month; it was another line on our to-do list but it was very important for my mother to visit and be close to him. But when I stand before his grave, I feel connected to him. I look at the stone and read the name "Edward D'arcy Clarity," with the dates of his birth and death. It is a reminder that he was and is no more. I am reminded he is gone and how much I miss him.

Our visit to his grave is followed by lunch at a cozy restaurant and we agree that a table close to the fireplace would be wonderful on this cold winter day. We welcome the roaring fire and and after a drink before lunch, we are warm and relaxed and able to enjoy the remains of the day.

Chapter

7

There were no discussions or formal plan as to who would do what for Grandma but we had a sixth sense, a perception of when we were needed.

For the most part, it was a labor of love but, as with every family, there would be some stress as to who was doing what and how often. The old house needed repairs in and out; during the summer months, the grass called to be trimmed and the winter snow required a strong back and willing arms. She would need a driver several times a week and we alternated between taking her to doctor appointments, labs, food shopping, and making certain she had a ride to Mass. There were a few bumps in the road but we fixed it and I don't think Grandma was ever aware of it.

As her years passed, she seemed to be content only when she was close to home and that was frustrating to the sisters. It would be difficult to keep her safe and healthy during the long winter months. She was frail and felt the cold at the slightest drop in temperature. The North wind would blow without compassion but with an uncouth velocity around the house, making it impossible for her to venture outdoors for days.

Each Christmas, Michael's gifts to Grandma would include an airline ticket to visit him in Hawaii. She would reluctantly accept his offer but was always anxious to return home. It was liberating for us to know that she would escape another Northeast winter and let the Oahu sun warm her bones. The other branch of the Clarity family would take good care of her and keep her busy.

Grandma and Bud were no strangers to Hawaii. They spent many winters in Hawaii, staying just a short distance from Michael's house. Michael's military status offered them a very interesting social winter, unique to a New York January. His friends became their friends.

I never could understand her reluctance to leave home. We thought it would be easy for her to return to Hawaii. This was her second home. Besides the obvious, spending time with Michael, Mary, and the girls, there was so much of Bud waiting for her in Oahu but then maybe that was the problem.

There were many phone calls from Hawaii; she would talk of the abundance of flowers and the beauty of the majestic green mountains that seem to join with the sea, the site of their violent birth. She described the opera that she enjoyed with Michael and she was laughing as she explained a movie she saw with Alice that was definitely not PG-rated. But in spite of her diverse days, there was always a sadness in her voice and I just did not get it.

As we talked, I was watching the snow accumulating in the driveway, knowing that it would soon be impossible to get the car out of the garage. I also knew that the afternoon would include several hours with a snow shovel.

This nasty winter had already produced several strong storms. One of these memorable events was a northeaster that brought unusually high tides and strong winds that carried large ice chunks that threatened her house. During the night, I could hear our oil burner running. It never seemed to stop and I whispered a silent prayer that it wouldn't.

I banished a vision of sunset over Diamond Head when she mentioned how homesick she was. I considered sending her some graphic images of dirty snow piling high in the streets and sidewalks already narrow from the shoveled mess. Frozen parkas and gloves were defrosting in preparation for the next call to snow duty and, of course, don't forget the lovely runny red noses. I found it hard not to lose my patience.

I should have realized that she had never been to Hawaii without Bud. Except for labor and delivery, there were few places she had ventured without him.

It had to be difficult to return to the places that they had shared together. Every vista and breathtaking beach offered another special and yet painful memory of the times they spent together. It would never be the same without him.

Soon after she died, I found several of her recent journals. Her four children were gathered in our childhood home for the difficult task of removing the possessions of a lifetime.

I went through some of her books and chose a few that were her favorites. My intention was to keep them in a place that would have pleased her. Included with these were several years of her personal journals..

I have always questioned what to do with journals: when do you discard them? I thought if a journal was intended to be forever private, one would assume that the author would ultimately destroy these private pages.

On the other hand, if it is the intention to preserve the writings indefinitely, does the author subconsciously hope that it would reach the eyes of her children, leaving to them their ultimate inheritance? Did these personal books become a venue for my mother to share her dreams and fears, her joys and disappointments, and speak to us, unashamed in a way that was impossible when she was alive.

After careful consideration, I decided to read some of Grandma's journals. Her handwriting was difficult to decipher and most of her pages, written in some recent years after Bud's death, were a record of some very ordinary days.

That is until I opened a book that went back to the years of her trips to Hawaii, the first as a recent widow. It was her thoughts written during this first trip.

The solitary line told it all; it was written as she first arrived in Hawaii. It read, "I just wanted to scream as we drove down these familiar streets. These were our places, the special drives we loved to take."

Her sister, Aunt Tootsie and my Uncle Jimmy were in Hawaii during her stay and they did have some pleasant visits but it was not an easy adjustment for her to no longer be half of a couple.

She missed the comfort of sharing each day with him and savoring the routine of the ordinary. Entering a favorite restaurant, he would know where she preferred to sit and she would browse the menu and point out that his favorite fish, Ono, was on the menu.

They enjoyed a quiet sunset, not knowing what to expect, but if they were disappointed, tomorrow would bring another. Bud appreciated her love of music, especially the opera, and he would be quiet, knowing not to chat during a special aria. She would give him all the time he needed with his camera, patiently sitting, waiting for the perfect light. If they were planning a trip, she took care of reservations and packed the bags which he would ultimately carry. To travel without him was to know he was gone.

On one occasion when we talked about her visits to Hawaii, she told me she never missed Bud when she was at home. There she was boarded by comforting memories in what would always be their home, the rooms she loved and where they raised their family.

Chapter

8

Grandma was a brave lady in spite of the few anxieties she would always carry with her. She had built her life on the edge of a bay and was a veteran of many severe storms, long before Bud came into her life.

After they married, she moved even closer to the threat of a tidal surge but it was a rare occasion when she left her home for a simple hurricane. The hurricane of 1938, that infamous storm that raised the bar for every storm to follow, found Grandma alone except for one companion, her young son, my brother Michael. She nervously watched with him as the blue sky with soft white cumulus clouds changed to an ominous shade of gray and then the darkest black she had ever witnessed. How frightening it must have been for my young mother to watch the water rise, moving close to the door, and the winds continue to grow stronger. Marguerite would take her son to a safer place, accepting the hospitality of her neighbors, the Howards.

They were safe with Mr. and Mrs. Howard in their large brick house, built on higher ground. She may have found shelter, but this was no hurricane party; she would make idle chatter and play with her baby but she would never stop worrying about her family and home. The storm had arrived as a "cat-3" with recorded sustained winds of 128 mph and a tidal surge of ten to twelve feet. It would finally pass as all storms do and when it was safe to return, her prayers were answered, and her beloved home was still standing, waiting to comfort her.

Every year, the bliss of a lazy, hot summer day is interrupted by the reality of tracking another hurricane heading up the East Coast. Families sit glued to the radio, waiting for an updated weather report, and follow the progress of Carol, Donna, Bell, or Grace. These female storms conceived in the waters off Africa, travel across the Atlantic, and give birth somewhere in the Caribbean Sea.

Sebastian Junger, author of *The Perfect Storm*, describes the perfect storm as a northeaster and a hurricane coming together at the same location at sea, at the same time. The people of Broad Channel have a different definition of the perfect storm. That would be the storm that hits New Jersey and spares New York.

Anyone who has lived in Broad Channel has bragging rights to a time when they hunkered down to ride out a nasty squall, nor'easter, or hurricane and lived to tell about it.

My parents' experiences on Jamaica Bay prepared them for some rough seas in other waters. Bud's first boat, the *Slow Poke*, as the name suggests, was an vetern twenty-three-foot wood boat with a small cabin and an engine that was not overpowered. They loved their boat. Bud would spend the spring season scraping and painting, getting it ready for another season.

He would take a "sick day" to work on his *Slow Poke* and then report to work the next day with red eyebrows and blue ears, the colors of his vessel. The boat was always ready for a June launching and the season's maiden voyage. Provisions and charts would be brought aboard — warm clothing, cameras, and the makings of a few Manhattans, stored in the cabin. They were ready to set out; this year their destination was the port of Albany.

One precruise storm occurred when Rosanne and I were shanghaied onto the *Slow Poke* and no matter how I carried on, I was on board that boat leaving Broad Channel and heading north up the Hudson River.

I was six months into my eleventh year and carried a sour face and enough comic books to sustain myself for the voyage. I am not sure when I began to enjoy myself but, whenever it was, I made sure to keep it to myself.

We left the waters of Queens County, and cruised uneventfully through the narrows that separated the boroughs of Staten Island and Brooklyn. The Statue of Liberty, that incredible symbol of freedom, bid us a welcome as we entered the Lower Manhattan Bay. The towering structures, known as the Manhattan skyline, were on our right and our boat suddenly seemed to shrink around us. The buildings appeared to form a wall around the city that reminded me of the gates that once protected the ancient biblical cities. Soon after we entered the Hudson River, Bud carefully guided our tiny craft alongside a massive ocean liner, the beautiful *SS United States*. With amazing timing, the door meant for the ship's pilot opened and a crew member handed out a bottle of wine, a gift for Bud. New York City was at times just a small town.

A short distance up the river, the *Mayflower II* rested in port. The beautiful ship had successfully repeated the awe-inspiring 1620 journey of the first and historic *Mayflower*. *The Mayflower II* sailed from England on April 20, 1957, and arrived in Providence, Rhode Island, following almost all of the original *Mayflower* route. The ship sailed under the command of Captain Allan Villiers; it was a very exciting crossing watched by the entire world.

After a proper sabbatical, the *Mayflower II* would sail to the port of New York City for an extended visit. My brother Michael, was among a group of midshipmen from Kings Point Military Academy on Long Island selected to sail on the ship from Providence to New York City, each taking their turn at the wheel. Captain Villiers and his crew were given a ticker-tape parade by the City of New York, a city that certainly knows how to host a parade.

The June weather was wonderful and I soon fell in love with the beautiful Hudson River. Just a few miles north of the city, we passed the lovely New Jersey Palisades, the sharp hills that border the river on our left, with colorful tug boats and barges passing on our right. The land divided by the river was pastoral and I envied the people who worked and who lived along the riverfront. We swam in the river, and soaked up the sun as we dried off on the deck while eating our lunch. We would each take a turn at the wheel, giving Bud a chance to enjoy his lunch.

I was into my third comic book as we approached the Tappan Zee Bridge and the idyllic day began to change. The rudder broke at the same time the river lost its calm and whitecaps began to circle our small boat. The sun began to set, darkness was replacing the security of sunlight, and cell phones were not yet even a prop in a James Bond movie. We were at the point of allowing ourselves to express fear when a good Samaritan offered to tow us to shore. We spent the night in a local motel and the next day the boat was repaired and we were ready to continue our journey.

A few years later, the *Slow Poke* was replaced by a bigger boat, the *Dream Boat*. She was twenty-eight feet long and very sea-worthy. The name was definitely influenced by their love of the new craft; it was their dream.

The maiden voyage of their Dream Boat was a trip up the Connecticut River. Their charts took them through Hellgate into the Long Island Sound and north up the river.

Hellgate is a narrow strait in the East River and, as the name suggests, could test the best of sailors. The name was derived from a Dutch word that meant "Hell's hole." The channel, lined with rocks, accounted for numerous shipwrecks over the years and after many attempts to remove the rocks, the channel was finally cleared by using explosives. Today, the main threat to sailors is the strong tides and commercial traffic. Although it was clear sailing through Hellgate, they did face many memorable storms along the Hudson.

There were several storms that defied their courage but with the arrival of another spring, they would begin to make plans for their next voyage.

As a widow, she spent many nights alone in her home during the violent storms; the wind would howl as the tides continued to threaten her security. I would call to suggest that she spend the night with us. We should pick her up before the tide surge prevented Ted from getting down her street. I wasn't very surprised when she calmly assured me she was fine and would prefer to stay and sleep in her own bed.

They were frequent fliers when airline travel was (excuse the pun) just getting off the ground. They began their adventures in the late '50s when air travel was both a glamorous and thrilling adventure available almost exclusively to the wealthy.

They flew first class on Eastern, Pan American, TWA, and their favorite, Air Lingus , to exotic places around the world as guest of the airlines. Passengers were pampered in flight by smiling, beautiful stewardess, wined and dined and deplaned with complimentary gifts, without a thought to terrorism.

It would be many years before a terrorist bomb brought down Pan American flight 103 over Lockaberbie, Scotland, in 1988. Two hundred and seventy lives were lost. It changed our lives and airline travel forever.

They did experience one white-knuckle flight returning from their eighth trip to their ancestral home of Ireland. An hour after the flight, the plane lost an engine and returned to Dublin. After a change of equipment, they resumed their journey and made a safe landing in New York. She remained anxious for several days but she eventually dismissed it and relived it only when it became interesting cocktail party conversation.

Chapter

9

Her annual checkups became increasingly difficult. She would always remain a brave lady but test results and reports would become her Waterloo. She lived through several stressful and traumatizing years.

She was diagnosed with breast cancer at the same time Bud was facing his own battle with colon cancer. She had a lumpectomy and began weekly radiation treatments but her priority would be Bud and his chemo sessions.

Surgery followed Bud's diagnosis of colon cancer but his prognosis was not hopeful. Life went on as usual but a dark cloud would follow them everywhere.

If we thought that three months of relaxing in the therapeutic rays of the Hawaiian sun would heal him, we were so wrong. He returned home to New York very thin and his complexion was a sallow yellow. A visit to his doctor confirmed our worst fears: the cancer had spread to his liver and he was not expected to live more than four months.

They left the doctor's office and went off somewhere for lunch as though it were just like any other day, just the two of them. I don't know how they passed that afternoon; they knew it was the finale of their life together.

For his children, it was the day we learned of our father's fate; we knew he was dying very soon. I could not sleep that night; I did not want to disturb anyone, so I sat on the bathroom floor and cried alone for hours. I thought to myself, over and over, *I don't want him to die.*

Our days were divided among praying, crying, and driving him to his chemo treatments. Their time alone at night had to be the most difficult for both of them.

He continued to live his life as he always had, with courage and humor. He enjoyed the family, danced at Danny and Ellen's wedding, and managed to keep interested in photography. His neighbors would always keep an eye on Bud Clarity's house, ready to be there for him when the time came. Our lives were changing and the roles reversing.

A man and woman who were a couple for over fifty years — it was almost impossible to imagine one without the other and yet the inevitable was looming on the horizon and we were not able to stop it.

These painful memories chase around in my head; my hopes are that after placing them on paper, they will tire and depart into a deep sleep. However, I will always recall one night that is especially painful to live with.

Grandma lived with chronic back pain and there were times when she was confined to bed rest for a few days. His cancer took a little more of him from us each day and then it was increasingly obvious. One night after work, I went to see them, bringing a dish of turkey soup for their supper. The house that had always been a sanctuary for me that night felt so different.

When I was small and if I was frightened, I was free to go into their room in the middle of the night, climb into their bed, and fall asleep between them. I needed them this very night to assure me that everything would be alright.

It was painful to look at my mother's eyes; she had been crying. It was the first time I saw her cry since Bud was diagnosed.

She looked very helpless when she asked me, "He is getting worse, isn't he?"

Bud came into the bedroom, carrying Grandma a cup of tea, and we chatted as though everything was fine; we were one in pretending for each other. It was a difficult ride home that night. This was the beginning of the end of a beautiful love story that began so long ago. They would always love each other but from a different place.

My father and I never really had lengthy conversations; I knew he loved me, but our conversations were usually just small talk. We were not a family of many words.

I don't know if he longed to talk to us for reassurance or to tell him that we would always be there for Grandma; I just didn't know how to begin.

I never told him I loved him or thanked him for a wonderful childhood. I would ask him every day how was he doing, did he need anything, could I do something, but I did not ask him if he was frightened or how I could take care of things for him in the future.

Maybe it was better this way; he knew that he was loved and maybe it was an escape for him to keep things the way they always were and talk to him about Pete Rose breaking a record.

The last months of his life, he was surrounded by love. We spent a beautiful afternoon together with Father Jack at his Hampton Bays cottage. Jack loved Bud; their friendship was special and we could count on Jack to say all the things to him that we were not able to.

Mary and Danny were in and out of my parent's house each day, making sure that things were being taken care of and if Bud needed anything. A special time for Bud was when they took him out on their boat for a tranquilizing cruise on the bay that had become such an important part of his life. He would feel close to God when he was so close to nature. He savored every moment.

Regina, Mike, with his great grandchild Jeanette brought Grandma Marguerite and Bud to the Catskills and we spent a few memorable days together. Bud borrowed Mike's car to take his bride of so many years for a last glimpse of their favorite Catskill vistas. Their marriage began in these beautiful New York mountains where they had spent their honeymoon and they would spend his twilight days where they had always been so happy.

They moved in the shadows of their chosen "Blue Mountains." He drove carefully around the gently winding roads that cut through lush, green fields. To the unknowing observer, it was a perfect August day; Queen Anne lace, daisies, and black-eyed Susans bordered the meadows and swayed to the rhythm of a gentle breeze.

I think he was at peace, spending some time alone, sitting in a rocker on our porch, inhaling the sweet aroma of the fresh cut hay that surrounded him. Muffin kept close to him, curled up and sleeping next to his chair, Bud might have prayed that time would stand still, if only for a few days.

The only sounds that interrupted his thoughts were coming from the field at the side of the house. He smiled when he recognized the laughter of Jeanette, being entertained by her Uncle Christian and Aunt Jackie.

A few neighbors passing in their pickups waved to him as he sat on the porch but Stanley, our friend and neighbor, pulled over and stopped to take time from his busy day to visit with Bud for a few minutes. Bud enjoyed his visits with Stanley; he loved the language of the farmer. Conversing as only good friends can, Stan talked with pride about his new tractor, complained about what a pound of mild was bringing, how many dry cows he had, and what fields would be turned over tomorrow. It gave Bud the connection to a way of life that city folks can only dream of.

I like to think that he thought as he sat alone on the porch, *This is a good day; I have lived a wonderful life and my family is a testament to this. God is good. This is a good day; tomorrow remains a mystery.*

Grandma and Bud spent a few nights with Rosanne and Bobby at their country cottage and she served him his favorite fruit, fresh local blueberries. After he died, we talked how something as simple as a favorite food could please Bud; it was a comforting memory.

Then a strange thing happened. Rosanne took a roll of exposed film from her camera to the supermarket for processing, not knowing that Bud had taken probably his last photograph with this camera. She wasn't sure what images were on the roll and she was curious when opening the envelope. Standing in the middle of the supermarket, she began to sob. Bud had photographed himself, smiling as he enjoyed his fresh blueberries, crème on top. He left Rosanne a thank-you message in a way he knew best.

My mother insisted on doing everything for him herself. He was approaching his last days and unable to leave his bed. His strong, handsome body was failing him and he was losing control of his bowels. The doctor had told Grandma that this was a sign that he was nearing his end. I went to see them and knocked before I opened the door. Grandma was very upset but she would not allow me to come in to help her. She insisted on it. I would always regret that I was not more assertive but I respected their privacy and his dignity. I will always feel there was something I could have done to help them that afternoon.

It was Labor Day weekend and I joined the others at Rosanne's house. We sat together on the deck and talked about Bud over a few drinks. It was a moment that only a family can share. Our sorrow was very real that day but slowly the alcohol took over and our mood changed from serious to somewhat giddy. I think that some hysteria took over, an early Irish wake.

I then looked across the water at my parents' house; I watched as he was placed in the ambulance that would take him away from us. She never told us he was leaving. We did so many things right but this we did wrong. I would always feel I failed but Grandma was in charge; it was her last act of love she would do for Bud and she protected his privacy. However, his children should have been there when he left his home for the last time.

I could not accept that he was not coming home. To see him in the hospital bed the next day, I finally came to terms that he was dying. Standing by his bed, I asked him, "How are you feeling, Bud?" He replied as though he was just down for a nap, "I feel just fine." He would never want to upset me; he would make it easy for us. I went out to the hall and cried quietly before I kissed him goodnight and went home. It was his last words to me.

He died alone that night. September of 1985 was not a time when you questioned laws and rules. When the hospital loud-speaker announced that visiting hours were over, we left. "Ours was not to wonder why, ours was to do and die." My father, without a squeeze of the hand or a kiss on the cheek, was left alone to enter the valley of death. He left us early on the morning of September 7.

Chapter

10

When the funeral was over, the sisters met at our mother's house to help sort through his belongings. It would be our final personal link to Bud, the last physical connection. We worked quietly, folding and organizing. We made an effort to maintain a casual demeanor, keeping our conversation light, but we failed when we came across his New York Press Photographers press pass, his rosary, and the family photos he carried in his wallet.

When we had finished except for a few things that Grandma could not part with, we joined her for a bit of refreshment, a glass of wine or whatever would help to erase the memory of the day.

As the wine mellowed our mood, we resorted to the wonderful gift of Irish humor to end the day with a smile. Grandma had just lost her best friend but not her sense of humor. Her daughters, fortified with a wicked, dark sense of humor, were ready to offer a good laugh, if necessary at the expense of someone else.

I don't remember who began but it was all about the limo driver. Mary has a wonderful laugh and always inspires a good witty story. Rosanne laughs loud and long, recognizing humor and embracing it whenever it presents itself. My mother would cover her mouth and her narrow shoulders would shake.

The next subject of our session was my Aunt Mary. We all loved her but she was the sacrificial lamb that we needed at that moment. Aunt Mary stood at her brother's coffin, protecting him with the patience of a sentry, and also took her role to meet and greet very seriously. A well-dressed man of about my father's age approached the coffin and introduced himself to Mary as a friend of Ed from the *Daily News*. The man stood quietly, with a polite respect for her habit, for what probably seemed to him an eternity listening to Mary's endless chatter before we found it necessary to run interference and rescue him.

He either needed a bathroom or a chair, maybe both; his eyes seemed to be crossing and I think he was on the verge of tears. My brother Michael stepped in and told Mary she was needed immediately in the other room. Feeling very important indeed, Mary finally released him. The man, grateful but puzzled, asked me if she was speaking in tongues.

We continued, each contributing a story, embellishing it for the right effect and Grandma jumped right in, making a difficult day a little easier.

The house would always remain exactly the way it was when he was there; the familiar walls around her kept his presence close to her. Each room was a shrine to his memory, the living room a testament to his talents. Plaques and certificates hung on every available space, awards presented by the New York Press Photographers Association, *Look*, and *Life Magazine*, and too many others to mention. The one he was most proud of was his special award for his contribution to the Pulitzer Prize awarded to the *Daily News*. His certificate was signed with an impressive note from the publisher, "Ed, we could not have done it without you."

She would sit in her chair, saying her prayers, her faith empowered by the magnificence of God's beautiful sunset. A glass of wine had now replaced her Manhattan and she looked forward to reading a new book by a favorite author that Mary had left for her. Tonight, if she had trouble sleeping, she would place her face to his pillow and drift off to sleep as if he were still there.

She told me shortly after he died that she made a promise to God that if Bud did not suffer, she would not burden her children with her grief. She did her best to keep that promise. I was naïve to think that she was even a little happy or content.

Chapter

11

My mother never had another reoccurrence with cancer but it would haunt her for the rest of her days. She had stored her fear in the canyons of her subconscious during the days that she was caring for Bud, but when he was gone, she allowed it to surface.

She would no longer be the center of a universe. The circle of life has levels of succession; parents are ultimately replaced by husbands or wives, and children in the line of family order. It must be that way, otherwise how would we manage to say good-bye? She began to crumble emotionally, despite the attention she received, as we tried to fill the emptiness in her life. Her depression matured slowly until over time it finally consumed her.

Rosanne and Bobby had moved shortly after Bud's death but she spent many hours with Grandma on the phone. Rosanne was a good listener and verbalized with compassion what Grandma needed to hear. Mary was the first call Grandma Marguerite made when she needed something and we took over her doctor visits. Ted had offered to drive her wherever and whenever she had an appointment.

Michael was going through his own personal hell; Mary Alice was in the last stages of her lengthy battle with breast cancer. She was leaving Michael, whom she adored, and her three daughters, for whom she fought so courageously during those crucial years of their teenage lives. It was more than courage; it was a determination that every mother would understand. It was vital that she attend Shelly's graduation or send them off with a smile to a sweet sixteen party or prom. She had to be there to offer a shoulder to a daughter who was having the normal teenage blues.

Our family was bonded in grief once again but Mary Alice's death affected Grandma in a very different way. Her loss of Bud, her breast cancer, and the tragic death of Mary Alice had just pushed her over the edge. Her world was spinning out of control and she did not have the strength or will to stop it. The energy to fight had just seeped out of her; she was on the cusp of a full breakdown.

At first we did not recognize it as depression. She had so many different symptoms; it was difficult to identify what had her so ill. Worried and confused, I turned to a close friend, Dr. Cranin, and he admitted her to the hospital.

She was seen by several doctors who all concluded that she was in good health. She returned home without an appetite or the ability to laugh or smile. She lost all interest in everything that had always made her happy. We waited patiently to see some sign of our mother returning but for several months she remained sad and withdrawn.

Mary Alice had a best friend, Gloria, and during her illness she and Michael had stayed in touch. He gave her updates on her friend's condition. He continued to call Gloria after the death of Mary Alice. Mary Alice, with a final act of love for her husband, strongly encouraged him to see Gloria after she was gone. She was adamant that Michael call her; she knew they would both need a friend.

The phone calls continued; Michael was mourning his wife and they shared a common loss. Eventually, together they booked a cruise.

When the news reached the sisters, the phone would be hot for days. We were not very fond of Gloria and we could never endorse her as a wife for Michael and thought it was not such a good idea for Gloria either.

Eventually, Michael and Gloria went their separate ways but it had nothing to do with the sisters' opining. There were two happy endings to this saga: the first, Michael married Mary, a perfect choice, and the second, Grandma was back to being Grandma again. A mini family soap opera, oozing with stimulating conversation mixed with a bit of gossip, was just what she needed.

Chapter

12

Perhaps if she knew how painful those twelve years as a widow would be, she would have tried to love him less. She was eighty-four when she fell in her kitchen and it was the beginning of her approaching demise. She tried very hard to regain her strength, only because she knew important to her children.

She would have dinner with us frequently and one night after dinner, I walked her out to the car and as we said our goodnights, she held my hand and said to me, "You are a wonderful daughter." I answered her, "You are a wonderful mother." We both knew it was the first of our last goodbyes.

It was her heart that failed her or maybe it was her accomplice; she was tired of trying to be happy. Her final year had her in and out of the hospital several times. In April of 1997, she was admitted for what would be the last time. Maybe we were naïve or in denial but we believed that she would be back home in just a few days.

She was not alone these days; there was always a steady stream of visitors each afternoon. Jackie, would visit her in the evening on her way home from work. She pampered her Grandma as they had their supper together.

The hospital room was filled with visitors the day she died. There was no plan; maybe the Lord had arranged it. We were now comfortable to bend a few hospital rules and her visitors exceeded the tolerated number.

She was animated and happy to see us. It was a festive party; the hostess wore blue and greeted everyone with a kiss. We were all talking at once, as we usually do, but a few had their eyes turned to the television, watching a tennis match. Her cookies were passed around but Daddy had his eye on her lunch. She gave her opinion of Tiger Woods and had a prediction for her beloved Yankees. An hour passed quickly and she said she would try to nap. We kissed her goodbye and, while she slept, she left us to join Bud.

For a second time, I would regret that I had left a parent to die alone but this time I was a bit easier on myself. She was not in pain and although her heart was failing, I don't believe she expected to die that day; she was planning to return home.

She had held court from her bed, surrounded by love, wearing her blue satin bed jacket to hide the drab hospital gown. She was in control, looking pretty, and speaking with her usual wit to those she loved. She died holding on to everything that was important to her.

On a beautiful May morning when the fragrance of lilacs fills me with joy, I am reminded of my mother. She was my mother and a best friend. She did all the parenting and she did it with a wonderful sense of humor. I loved to see her laugh; she did it so well.

Our parents were not perfect; they had some thunderous fights and small explosions that could be very upsetting for the rest of our family. They occasionally disappointed me and there were many times I felt isolated and alone. This could be anyone's story: parents acting as ordinary people and, in spite of this, their children in turn becoming ordinary people. Our families happy memories far outnumbered the bad. They molded the template for our lives and I was happy to swim in their wake.

The grief that followed their death had different plateaus. Some days the pain is more acute and over time it does subside. But that sadness is a testament to how much they were loved.

Chapter

13

One evening following my mother's funeral, I sat very alone, watching a movie, when a wave of melancholy swept over me. I then experienced a lovely sensation of a soft touch to my face. It startled me but I was certain that it was my mother letting me know she was still there for me.

I thought about it for days and it brought back a memory of a night a long time ago. Rosanne and I shared a bedroom but that night I was also alone, except for my blanket.

My blanket was a very important part of my childhood. I called it my "nice blanket" but that definitely was a euphemism. My companion was not a soft cuddly blanket that shows up at baby showers; it was actually very pathetic. There were no union label nor was it hypoallergenic, fireproof, and safe by all government standards. It was striped with dark, dreary shades of brown. It was stitched down each side and resembled a very large pillow case or a sleeping bag for a short, fat adult.

When I was a toddler, it was never far from my side and it remained with me, even accompanying me on my high school senior trip to Washington. Daddy suggested I take it with me to the hospital when I went into labor with Regina. I wasn't sure that it would be welcomed in a sterile area so reluctantly I left it home.

We did have one premature separation and that would be when my brother Michael threw the blanket into the canal right behind our house. I actually witnessed my security blanket floating in the water. After I expressed just the right amount of horror to get my mother's attention, she sent him out to salvage it although he denied he was guilty.

I will never know who ordered the separation but maybe they thought it was the right thing to do. Today it might be called an intervention. I was angry and traumatized at the time but, in hindsight, maybe it was time; I was just short of nine years old.

The night of my memory I was about three years old, sitting up in my bed with the blanket, and crying like my heart would break. Maybe I was having a meltdown, I don't know, but I remember the sadness I was feeling. My mother came up the stairs, probably leaving the dinner dishes in the sink, and just sat on my bed. She never lost her patience or said a word. It was dark and quiet, just me, my blanket, and my mom. Eventually I fell asleep, maybe sad but not alone.

As you all know, I was born on the eleventh of January, 1944. I don't think my birth could have been planned. Although I followed a boy and a girl, the perfect family, I have no doubts about my being wanted but I am sure it was a surprise. It was just the timing; why would you plan a child who would make an appearance just two weeks after Christmas?

My parents' conversation might have been something like this: "Let's have our next baby in January. We might have just enough time to take down the Christmas tree and find a place for the gifts. Oh, and we will need the bassinette. We can take it down when we bring the decorations up."

There would be prayers for clear skies, hopes that there would not be two feet of paralyzing heavy snow or a Nor'easter that would flood the streets. My mother probably thought about the possibility of the draw bridge that connect us to the hospital on the mainland freezing in the up position.

If it were up to me, January would not have been a month I would have chosen for my grand entrance. Most friends and family are not anxious to return to the mall for a birthday gift after six weeks of intense Christmas shopping and returns. If they do venture out, the stores are void of inspiration.

The shelves are as empty as the average shopper's bank account. When I was old enough for a birthday party, twenty-five of my closest friends were invited and rescheduled according to the January weather. Beautifully decorated birthday cakes went untouched when the streets were covered with two feet of snow.

Then there is the annual New Year's resolution diet, which usually lasts no more than two weeks from the beginning of the New Year. That works out to three days after my birthday. The offer of a slice of birthday cake will cause the same adults who consumed enough calories during the Christmas season to sustain a pregnant elephant to recoil in horror at the sight of a single slice of birthday cake. It is just depressing.

While I am on the subject of my birth month, the day of the week was not so great either; I was born on a Tuesday. When I was old enough to understand the poem, The Mother Goose rhyme "Monday's Child Rhyme" was read to me. I wasn't too thrilled to learn that Tuesday's child was full of grace. I would have preferred Monday. Monday's child is fair of face.

My arrival on Tuesday, however, is preferred to arriving on Wednesday, whose child is full of woe. I could have gone through life woeful if my birth was delayed by a few hours.

A mid-January birth also has the distinction of having the Zodiac sign of the Capricorn. Anyone familiar with Capricorns must know how boring and practical they are. The distinction of inviting just one Capricorn to your party will guarantee the party to be an absolute failure. Nineteen years later, I married another Capricorn, which meant two boring souls attending the same party. I have worked very hard at losing this stigma, maybe a little too hard.

So without much fanfare, another Clarity entered the world, Marguerite Mary Clarity. It was an uneventful occasion since I never heard of anything to the contrary. No blizzard or floods were responsible for the blessed event taking place at home nor did I take my first breath in a rowboat on a flooded street. And so it began, the first nineteen years of my life living on Fifteen Road in Broad Channel.

Chapter

14

Broad Channel, a small island, about one mile in length, sits in the middle of the beautiful Jamaica Bay. Hundreds of years before Rosanne and I, along with our faithful dog Curley, played cowboys and Indians along the shoreline of the bay, the Canarsie and Jameco Indian tribes fished and hunted these same waters. As the years went by, large numbers of immigrants arrived and settled in New York City and the city would become known as the "melting pot." It was only a matter of time before the fishermen followed the catch and found their way to the waters of Broad Channel. The boats and poles changed with the years but their ultimate rewards remained the same, returning home with a boat filled with shrimp, crabs, and fish.

Somewhere around the middle of the 1800s, fishing shacks and stations began to surface on the island. With shelter from the sun and storms, the fishermen began to bring their families and slowly a seasonal port began to form.

The most important event to contribute to the formation of a town was the Long Island Railroad. In 1881, Broad Channel became a station of the railroad and there was no turning back. Broad Channel would become the Atlantis rising from the sea, with the immediate area closest to the railroad station becoming the hub of the hamlet.

Hotels catering to the fishermen appeared and soon it became a summer colony boasting lodging, music, food, and drink, and of course swimming and fishing.

It was about this time that the family of Martin Gronachan left Sligo, Ireland, to escape the famine and poverty of Ireland and immigrated to Canada.

Martin Gronachan would never be described as dull or boring; he was a most unusual man. He was, to his grandchildren, larger than life. He was born in Toronto and when he was two years old, the family moved to Buffalo. Years later, something, maybe fate, brought him to New York City and Theresa Sullivan, my grandmother. Theresa was as quiet as Pop was loud and she was petite as he was burly.

Grandma Theresa described her ethnic background as a Beara Sullivan. The Beara is a wild and rugged Irish peninsula; it is surrounded by the beautiful Bantry Bay on one side and the Atlantic Ocean on the other. Sparsely populated cliffs and grazing meadows are dotted with sheep farms and small, quaint towns.

Dad and I visited the Beara on our second trip to Ireland. We had a vivid introduction to the philosophy of Irish life when we set out to rent a car. We had completed the forms and studied the maps when we noticed the tires were worn and we were naturally concerned as they did not appear to be safe. We did not want to offend the lovely man in the rental office, so in our best "we are not arrogant Americans" tone of voice, Dad mentioned the tires to the agent. He replied, "Aye, I will light you a candle" as he handed us the keys and walked away.

Off we went, camera and maps on hand, and confident that the candle would burn for at least two weeks. We drove the Beara, or Dad drove and I prayed.

It was definitely a white-knuckle road trip but an exciting one. We had previously driven many miles in Ireland but the infrastructure in this area was definitely a challenge.

At the tip of the peninsula, the road narrows, with large boulders bordering on each side of the rough road. We followed one sharp turn after another and, at one point, I slowly removed my hands from my eyes to see the reason for Dad's swearing; it was excessive even for him.

I joined him with a few of my own favorite words when I spotted a brightly painted car with large numbers displayed on each door. The vehicle was approaching us at great speed and I managed to get a glimpse of the very intent driver. He narrowly missed us as he took the turns on two wheels. We were sharing the wrong side of the road and it was obvious that this driver claimed both sides. It was at this moment that I realized that we were sharing the road with an Irish auto race.

Somewhere in the middle of these suicide drivers was a legally blind, ninety-year-old farmer's wife on her way to the market or the pub, whichever came first. She was holding her own. Eventually the race was behind us and the terrain was a bit easier.

We resumed the tour, amused that we were worried about bald tires, and we began to enjoy the view around us. The mountains that tower over the Atlantic Ocean are surrounded by rolling green fields, home to herds of grazing sheep. We noticed that each farm identified their herd by painting on the back of every animal a specific shade of bright paint.

We gazed down on the wild sea crashing against the rocks before we noticed a quaint farm just up ahead. It was a pastoral scene commonly found in travel brochures — that is until we noticed the barn yard filled with sheep and the gate to the yard was opened wide.

Inside the fence stood a group of innocent teenage sheep, pretending not to notice their potential path to freedom. They feigned a look of absolute sleepy contentment. I began to regret the pleasure I experienced the night before at dinner, a perfect rack of lamb, cooked rare with a crusty coating and served with mint jelly.

We prided ourselves as the good American tourists and pulled over at the farm house to warn the farmer. As quickly as an Irishman is genetically able to respond, he summoned the dog with a call to duty: round up the sheep that were actually not so content any longer.

I heard them before I saw them. I raced to the safety of the car, which was the only thing that separated me from this large herd of racing beast. They divided, each platoon taking one side of our vehicle. I believe they were inspired by the Irish car race that flew by a few minutes earlier. They seemed to be looking sheepishly through the car window as they galloped past us. I swear I saw one wink at me.

The dogs did an excellent job of rounding up these joyful truants. The sheep were incarcerated once more, the barnyard was locked, and as we waved goodbye to the farmer, we heard him mumble something about needing a Guinness.

This was not the last that we saw of the backside of the Irish sheep. It would seem that with every turn in this endlessly winding landscape, we would come to a complete stop by yet another group of these meandering creatures. I began to sense that they enjoyed their authority over the road. They were a living, breathing road block—a stop sign covered with fur and attitude.

Chapter

15

Grandma Gronachan was a pretty young woman with long silky curls. She was proud of being a Manhattan girl, living in the Bowery. I assume she was also proud to marry Pop, Martin Gronachan, since she agreed to move to Buffalo, his hometown. She gave it a try but Buffalo was too cold and had so much snow and eventually they returned to New York City and she was happy to be a New York City girl again.

My grandfather would take advantage of any opportunity the city had to offer. Lacking a high school diploma, he depended on his brawn and chutzpah to support his family.

Pop was a legend in Broad Channel. When I was growing up, a neighbor speaking about my grandfather told me that Martin Gronachan was the strongest man he had ever met. His strength and muscles were overshadowed only by his gift of gab. He would approach a job site and was able to convince the foreman that he was the most qualified man for this particular project. After one such interview, he was hired to join the crew on the construction of the Manhattan Bridge.

The construction of the bridge began in 1901 and was completed in 1909. He loved that bridge and he was very proud to be part of it but to hear him tell it, he was single-handedly responsible for its creation and completion.

When the bridge was finally completed, Pop would move on to the next opportunity. Martin Gronachan would not be another Irishman on the dole.

It has been said that the Irish immigrant had a very difficult time in finding employment after arriving in New York. My parents never spoke of the old country or our Irish background; it wasn't trendy to reminisce about where you had been but rather brag about where you were going.

My family was neither ashamed nor proud of being Irish; they were Americans, born in New York. Occasionally, however, there was some talk about their grandparents and how difficult it was to find a job when they arrived from Ireland. I listened to them speak about the "Help Wanted" signs that hung in various establishments and next to them the "NINA" signs, which stood for "No Irish Need Apply."

I was never aware that I was Irish until I was maybe six years old and we were getting an oil delivery. It must have been a slow play day; I watched as the delivery man connected the hose to the house, making sure he got it right. I think I made him nervous; he began to make small talk and asked me my name. When I told him Clarity, he replied, "So you're Irish." I was truly shocked; no one ever told me I was anything but American. My grandparents, with the exception of Pop, who was born in Canada, were all born in the United States. It would be many years before we discussed our Irish heritage.

When I was a teenager, it was so cool to be Irish and to celebrate St. Patrick's Day in a very Irish Broad Channel. There was the annual bash at the parish hall, we all wore green, sang Irish ditties, and danced to the music of the day. Most of the guys, some of the girls, and most underage would drink green beer. The hall was filled with Irish, Irish wannabes, cigarette smoke, music, and the June Hartel dancers. That night we all were proud to be Irish until the green beer kicked in. I was always home before the police arrived to break up the fights and clear the hall.

Grandma and Bud would travel to Ireland a total of eight times; it became their favorite place outside of Broad Channel and the Catskills. After arriving in Ireland, it does not take longer than the time to drink a Guinness to fall in love with this beautiful land.

Chapter

16

There are some historians who do not agree with the authenticity of the NINA signs. They argue that women could easily find work as domestics or nannies. Men, they point out, found many opportunities in the high-mortality jobs: firefighters and policemen, especially in the cities of New York, Boston, and Chicago. The immigrants also worked on canal projects and railroads but they stayed away from farm work. The generation of farmers that preceded them came close to extermination due to the famine.

There were gangs, formed for protection, unity, and strength on job sites. The Irish did look kindly on the drink, and gang drinking led to the Irish being stereotyped by many as violent and criminal. There were many arrests and it was said that the Irish arrestees' numbers equaled Irish arrestors.

One historian, George Potter, quotes a newspaper image of the Irish immigrant: "You will scarcely ever find an Irishman dabbling in counterfeit money, breaking into houses or swindling; but if there is any fighting to be done, he is very apt to have a hand in it. Even though Pat might meet a friend and for love knock him down, the fighting usually resulted from sudden excitement, allowing that there was but little malice prepense in his whole composition."

The Irish certainly found discrimination in employment, housing, and also in the public schools system. The St. James version of the Bible, which had derogatory referrals to Catholic, was used in the public school system, thus the creation of the Catholic schools.

The Irish fled to the United States a desperate, broken people and of the immigrants who sailed from Ireland in 1847, one in five died. They died of diseases that resulted from malnutrition, secondary to the famine. The holocaust known as the famine followed the Irish on their voyage to North America and as a result the ships that brought them here came to be known as coffin ships. The survivors, arriving in New York, were determined to overcome the horrors they left behind and build a new life that would feed their family.

The Great Famine — The Great Hunger

"The Almighty, indeed sent the potato blight, but the English created the famine."

History has taught us that civilized nations have acted in the most uncivilized manner. The Romans created Christian martyrs and fed them to the lions. The Egyptians had their slaves, the Jews, who were also Hitler's holocaust. Africans were taken from their homeland and shipped across the oceans as slaves for the white man; Saddam Hussein gassed the Kurds and the Irish suffered genocide under the British rule.

To understand the core of the Irishman's mind and soul, you must know about the famine.

Ireland was a conquered nation. It wasn't always that way. Long before a king sat on the throne in England, Ireland had a monarchy that ruled over a nation of many tribes.

Invasions, wars, and battles were repeated throughout Ireland over the years. The Vikings, most notably, invaded Ireland in the 800s and played a pivotal role in Irish history. In the early 1800s, it was England who directly governed Ireland, forming the United

Kingdom and abolishing the Dublin parliament. The strategy of Great Britain was to anglicize the Irish Catholics. Celebrating Mass was forbidden by the English, so secret caves replaced the churches. The Irish were also banned from holding public office, getting an education, or owning land.

The landowners of Ireland were the British aristocracy. The economy of these estates depended on the grain they sold to European countries. When the demand fell, the estates were living above their means and they were highly mortgaged.

The primary concern of the British government was not the poor and hungry of Ireland; it was the survival of the aristocracy. Many feel what followed was the plan of the Crown—that is to control and diminish the population of Ireland. They would use the failure of the potato crop as a means to accomplish their goal. Also, the British and the Europeans had a taste for beef. The green fields of Ireland, which had always been used for farming, were turned into pastures for beef cattle.

In order to clear the land for additional crops, the poor were evicted from their homes on the estates. Hundreds of peasants were homeless and wandered the streets as beggars. Others were given a small, one-acre plot to feed their family. The one crop that would grow in barren soil was the potato. It became the sole source of food for the Irish families. Their only sustenance was water and potatoes and then there was the blight that destroyed the entire potato crop for more than two years. All of these factors contributed to creating the famine, which began in 1845, and was then used as an attempt to destroy an ancient heritage and resulted in the death of one million people.

Families were starving. Parents were unable to feed their children and stood by and watched their babies die an agonizing death. Leon Uris, in his historical novel *Trinity*, explained the horror. The ditches of Ireland filled with the dead and dying. There were families who would walk together into the cemetery to ease the burden of their burial. Families would lay together, babies moaning, only skin stretched over their bones, covered with stinking sores and bloated from dropsy. Often one or more would be dead for days, lying in the arms of their parents.

During this time, the ports of Ireland were bulging with food. Ships loaded with beef and grain were set to sail abroad with enough food to save a nation. Fishing was forbidden; it was the gentry's land. Many historians would refer to this as genocide.

The government of the United Kingdom pursued a policy of mass starvation in Ireland with the intent to eliminate a substantial ethnic and racial group commonly known as the Irish people.

When the news of the atrocious conditions existing in Ireland reached the world, charity from abroad began to reach the Emerald Isle. Calcutta made the first donation of fourteen thousand pounds. Donations from rich and poor were sent to the Irish people. An American tribe, the Choctaws, sent their donation and Queen Victoria, the head of the United Kingdom, donated two thousand pounds.

In 1845, Ottoman Sultan Abulmecid declared his intentions to send ten thousand sterling and three ships of food. Queen Victoria requested that the Sultan send only one thousand because she had sent two thousand. He did send one thousand but he secretly also sent the three ships of food. The courts tried to block the ships but the food arrived safely at the Irish harbor.

So now you know what was present in the mind and soul of the Irish immigrant. To protect and feed their families, the gangs were formed, other victims took to the drink to erase the memories they brought with them to New York, and others, like Pop Gronachan, sought any opportunity to support his family. Pop was born thirty years after the worst of the famine but the past was always present.

Chapter

17

It is possible that it was fishing that brought Martin Gronachan to Jamaica Bay but it might have been the Hotel Enterprise that drew Theresa to Broad Channel.

The Enterprise was a three-hotel complex, connected by boardwalks and located bayside. The hotel offered dinner, drinks, music, and a place to visit with friends. It was a wonderful way to spend a hot summer Sunday afternoon, especially if you fished or just wanted to enjoy a swim. Maybe it was not one particular amenity but all of the above that led my grandparents to buy a small summer island home.

Their new vacation home could hardly be called a house; it was a two-room bungalow located on what was then called Jamaica Bay Boulevard but we know it today as Cross Bay Blvd. Pop had the little house moved to the middle of Eleventh Road. The Island was geographically a legitimate island in every sense, not connected to a mainland by a bridge. It was common for barges to deliver a house to Broad Channel and it would then be moved to a more desirable location. In time, canals were dug on the west side of Broad Channel and Pop now leased waterfront property outside his door and if the tide was very high, it might be inside his door.

Broad Channel in the early 1900s was an exciting place to spend the summer. As with any seasonal community, there was a party for every occasion and if there was no occasion, they would invent one. My grandparents enjoyed the time they spent on the island and took advantage of everything it had to offer.

On a beautiful summer evening, Grandma and Pop might walk the narrow boardwalk to the end of their road, each carrying a drink, to wait for the daily spectacle referred to as sunset over Jamaica Bay. On a quiet night, they might get together with their friends to watch a silent film at the movie dome, a Broad Channel outdoor cinema. Any day, when the sea was tranquil, Pop would fish for fluke or flounder and in the evening, he and Grandma Theresa might visit one of the local dance halls.

They had a new circle of island friends and a busy social life during those first summer weekends. Grandma would probably take her time getting herself ready for their night out. She brought a new dress with her from the city, and she would try something different with her hair. It was a very exciting moment when they entered the dance hall. The noise from both the music and the crowd made it difficult to talk and Pop would have to shout to the bartender to order their drinks. After saying their hellos and spending some time with Grandma, he might step out to the boardwalk, light a cigar, and talk to his cronies about the day's fishing. He would exaggerate about his catch but no more than everyone else. Well, knowing Pop, maybe a bit more.

A few stores had now opened for business and a volunteer fire department was in operation. A fire department needs a fire house and that would take some financing.

The first Broad Channel Mardi Gras was organized in 1908 on Labor Day weekend as a way of raising the funds. There were other options, a bake sale, an auction, but a Mardi Gras was very Broad Channel.

It would be the finest grand finale of their summer season. The Mardi Gras was a great success and over one hundred years and five generations later, the people of Broad Channel continue to parade down Cross Bay Blvd. on Labor Day.

Labor Day weekend Mardi Gras! What special memories I will always have of that annual celebration. In the weeks that lead up to it, the entire town is excited and will begin to make preparations. The local bars pick their candidates for the royal family: a king and queen, prince and princess, and of course a mayor.

Once the candidates are chosen, serious fund raising begins. Waterfront parties and tavern benefits are held throughout the summer and the profits will be turned over to the Broad Channel Volunteer Fire Department. The candidates that raise the most money will reign as the royal family for the Labor Day weekend.

Labor Day weekend approaches, the campaigning ends, and it is time to count the votes. This will be held in a neutral location under tight security. It rivals the counting of votes between George Bush and Al Gore but without the dangling chads. The competing rivals gather nervously, waiting for the result, and finally the winners are announced. The Broad Channel royal family is crowned and the celebration will last for the next three days. They have raised an impressive donation to the fire house building fund and will not so regally spend the weekend partying and consuming a large quantity of beer

The Mardi Gras officially begins on Saturday morning and two parades are scheduled: one by land and the other by sea. We walk quickly to Noel Road, hoping we haven't missed any of the baby parade. A crowd has formed and parents are lining up their floats after a slow start. We realize we had plenty of time. I always wonder at one of these events if the contestants will be in kindergarten before the parade begins. Moms fuss with their toddler's costume; others offer a pacifier to a crying infant and dads checks the integrity of the float. Then it begins; flags wave and there is a wall of cameras. It was worth the wait; each float is unique and the babies are beautiful but only one will win the first prize trophy.

I remember sitting on our fence enjoying the brisk September morning, happy to be free of the August humidity. I was eating a bowl of Cheerios while waiting for the parade to begin. Finally I spotted the flotilla of many different size boats. They cruised in formation past our house, each decorated with colorful flags and always the red, white, and blue. The American flag would fly a little higher than all the other flags as the boats cut a wake in the deep blue water. It gave me a sense of pride in my town, which has always been very patriotic.

I cannot remember any organized sports in Broad Channel when I was growing up with the exception of the Nut Club. This was a local football team for the teenage boys and young men. So the neighborhood looked forward to activities for the children: the running and swimming races during Mardi Gras.

I remember the one and only time I participated in a competitive sport. I entered a running race and it seems like yesterday that I stood on the hot, sandy field waiting for the signal to begin. Somewhere in the crowd, a voice amplified by a bull horn announced my race and my heart was pounding as I prepared to leave the starting line.

I evaluated my competition and when the gun went off, I ran like Forest Gump on a good day. The crowd was cheering but not for me. I came in second and I was presented with a medal but there were no family or friends to share my triumph. Well, I have heard it said by that wise philosopher Jerry Seinfeld that "second place is the first of many losers" but I was happy with my win, although I missed the support of my family.

Sunday was a fun full day; we spent it at the Broad Channel day camp. The owners of the camp opened the facilities to the town for the day and the pool was used for the Mardi Gras swimming races.

There were some very good swimmers in Broad Channel. Jamaica Bay was the only playground we knew. We all learned to swim very early; it was required if you lived just a few feet from the water. I did enter one swimming race without any significant result and I never took part in any competitive sport again.

We swam almost every summer day; I always loved the bay and also welcomed the challenge of the ocean surf but it was a rare occasion when we had an opportunity to swim in a pool. The water was a crystal-clear turquoise and when we swam under the water, we could actually see our feet. It was probably odd that I enjoyed the smell of chlorine and the rubber bathing caps, with their own distinguishing odor, but I have always associated memories with the sense of smell. We enjoyed being part of a group of children having fun.

Maybe it was the forbidden fruit that made it so attractive. My mother did her best to keep us away from crowds; she was very nervous that we would come in contact with polio, and she was not alone. For a few years, children throughout the country were kept away from swimming pools, movie theaters, and summer camp.

The polio epidemic in the '50s crippled thousands of children and traumatized a nation. There was no known cause or cure. Eventually it was believed that this plague was the result of improved sanitary conditions.

It was accepted that infants exposed to small amounts of the virus that lived in open sewers developed immunity and when the sewers were replaced, the epidemic broke out.

The children of Broad Channel attended St. Virgilius School and if New York City was a family, Broad Channel was the neglected child. Our parish buildings were surrounded by a green moat that carried open sewage. We became experts at jumping over the moat, most of the time. I was not aware of any of my schoolmates having polio.

The day camp was on the south side of the channel and every weekday during the summer, a caravan of yellow school buses brought hundreds of children through Cross Bay Blvd. and deposited them for whatever it is they do at day camp.

To us Broad Channel kids, camp was an anomaly. School was out and our days were free from structure. Our only schedule was the rise and the fall of the tide. We had no envy for the children of a world different than ours; we assumed that their parents would prefer them to be supervised somewhere far away from home.

On the other hand, it was not necessary to leave God' little acre. We thought we lived in the best place on earth. Our world was small, just one mile north to south, and our perimeters were measured by nautical miles. We were happy in our innocence and maybe that is all that is important.

When the races were over and the trophies handed out, it was time to prepare for the final event of the weekend, the parade.

Brainstorming always began at the eleventh hour; the think tank must create a theme for this year's float. Somehow it was a tradition to wait until the very last minute; their creative abilities obviously thrived on stress. A few ideas would be tossed around and finally they had a plan. Now it was time to make it come alive.

There was a rush for building materials, a flat-bed truck, music, and costumes. The girls went home to rummage through the attic trunks. They returned carrying props, makeup, and the makings for interesting costumes.

The guys were busy with their man tools, working up a thirst, as they molded their brainchild into, hopefully, a winning float.

It was now time to connect the sound system and attach the backdrops securely, making sure they wouldn't fall onto the street during the parade. Someone was designated to get rid of all the empty beer cans that had accumulated.

The scenario was repeated throughout town. The adrenalin was pumping as the competitive spirit grew by the hour. Rumors spread: was it true that Ninth Road was doing a Miss Rheingold Beer float? Information of the opposition's design and progress continued all morning. It would be difficult to win but even more difficult to lose.

It is Labor Day and the parade is scheduled to begin at noon. My contribution to this annual event would be that of a spectator and I was happy to do my part.

My mother would walk Rosanne and me to the Eleventh Road corner to watch the parade with my grandparents. We would leave a little early, anticipating that our annual stroll down Cross Bay Blvd. would take longer than on any other day. The houses were all decorated with streamers and flags of red, white, and blue. The sidewalks were crowded with folding chairs and in each chair sat a friend or neighbor of my mother, whom they called Mag or Marguerite.

Grandma Marguerite must have been very lonely in the crowd; she missed Bud more than usual on these holidays when she was surrounded by so many happy families.

We finally arrive at Eleventh Road and we see the familiar faces of our aunts and uncles and, most important, our cousins. Rosanne and I would be quick to join the cousins sitting on the curb, eagerly awaiting the parade.

There is much anticipation preceding the parade but in the distance we can see the lights of the fire truck and someone yells that they are about to begin but they are just hopelessly optimistic. Our front-row seats will give us a good view of the parade once it begins but, as the crowd assembles, we see only legs, many legs, all sizes and shapes.

Animated and loud adult conversation hovers above us. It is very much like the gobbling of turkeys, a Charlie Brown moment. There are so many tall legs and garbling noises up there; it is just a small world, after all.

The boulevard suddenly becomes a flurry of energy. The red Mars lights on the police cars signal to vehicles to merge into one lane while the vendors pushing their wagons are hawking balloons, toys, and more of tomorrow's trash.

Spectators become spectacles as they work their way across the boulevard carrying coolers, babies, and chairs to view the parade marching south. Several strange unidentifiable individuals, dressed in outlandish costumes, are running through the crowd in an attempt to meet their float.

It is a Labor Day tradition that the parade will not begin as scheduled and today that tradition will not be broken. Finally we hear the music and the flashing lights are moving closer to us. The parade has begun and the Broad Channel Volunteer Fire Department is approaching.

The bright red trucks have been washed and polished for the parade and slowly move down the parade route with loud air horns and sirens announcing their arrival. The crowd is excited except for the few leashed dogs, who are cowering under chairs.

The cousins look up with envy at the special children who sit in the fire engine cab throwing candy to the humble crowd and we scurry to pick it up.

The firemen always receive a loud ovation from the admiring crowd. They look handsome in their full dress uniform, marching close to their shiny trucks. These first responders are the heroes of Broad Channel. The residents recognize their valuable contribution to the town, knowing that the bridge that connects us to Rockaway also separates us from city emergency services when the draw bridge is up.

The fire department is followed by the marching band of St. Camillus. The music made by these talented teenagers fills the street with a festive and carnival ambiance. A small group of local politicians do the mandatory photo ops. They dress and walk politically correct as they give a slight twist of their hand that resembles a wave. The applause they receive will vary from year to year.

The politicians are followed by the members and families of the American Legion. They are greeted with the respect and warmth they deserve. There are salutes and waving flags in their honor. The scouts, from Brownies and Cub Scouts to the prestigious Eagle Scouts, march together in perfect unison under the flag.

Now the fun begins; the parade gets very interesting. The floats and walkers will not disappoint the crowd, they are clever and timely. There are funny political spoofs, parodies on current events, or just sheer silliness.

Our friends, family, and neighbors are quick to show their uninhibited side as they role play and move into character with the help of the few cases of beer that are always nearby.

The grand finale is the royal family entourage. I knew that it was just pretend; I just got swept away for the moment. The convertible cars, the faux ermine draping that looked so beautiful, the velvet robes, and the bejeweled tiaras and crowns fed my fantasy. I can see myself sitting on the back of the convertible, waving regally yet ever so kindly to my subjects while carefully adjusting my tiara for the photographers. I would be a kind and just queen.

Chapter

18

The parade is over, the chairs are folded, and the crowd heads to the final Labor Day event, the closing party. We hear car horns blowing in the distance, the celebratory, triumphant noise of the winning floats. The trophies have been awarded and the trucks with floats circle the town. They are waving their trophies and flaunting their victory until the crowd has left, their audience gone.

We assemble, parents gathering their children, and walk together to Grandma and Pop's house. If this was your first visit to my grandparents' house, you could be either impressed or depressed. If you were materialistic or a follower of the latest decorating trends, you would definitely not be impressed.

However, if you appreciate the avant-garde or your preference is cozy-quaint, then you could be impressed by my grandparents' home. It was originally a two-room bungalow and it grew with the family.

The sun porch, most likely, was added to the front of the house on a warm spring day when Pop was looking forward to summer entertaining. He wanted a spacious room to gather with their all their family, friends and neighbors. It was a large room for such a small house. Windows filled three walls, scattering morning sunlight throughout the porch. My Grandma Theresa might sit here in the early morning and enjoy the healing warmth of the sun on her body. She would read the morning newspaper as the world around her came back to life. The neighbors began to open their doors, reaching for the newpaper and the milk before it soured. Others would wave to her as they passed her windows on their way to work and soon it would be time for the children to make their way to school.

There would always be adequate seating whenever the family gathered together. The furniture was a rustic red and black Adirondack design with several rockers and small tables but the grandchildren's favorites were the gliding couch and chairs. This was an authentic family room filled with happy summer memories of bare feet, sunburned faces and crab traps left outside.

Her bedroom, a tributary of the small living room, was light and airy, dispersing sunlight into the otherwise light-deprived living room. The two rooms were divided by French doors that always remained open with a couch placed between the doors to create a border. It was a unique layout and it may have lacked privacy but it was an interesting alternative to watch television from the comfort of her bed.

As a little girl, I loved her bedroom. It was soft, feminine and very much her own space. The walls were a pale shade of peach, which complemented the dark, ornate bed covered with the same pale peach satin bedspread. If you were standing in the living room, with perfect lighting, her bedroom might be taken for a large painting that was placed over the couch. On the special nights when Rosanne and I slept over, we would share Grandma's bed. I enjoyed just being in her room, looking with curiosity at her favorite things, especially the treasures she kept on her dresser.

You can tell quite a bit about a lady by the personal things she selects to place on her dresser. There was a small framed sketch of a black cat that was given to my Grandma by a nine-year-old artist, my sister Mary. A large bottle of Apple Blossom cologne sat conveniently for her daily dab and her jewelry box that held colorful brooches and her infamous pearls sat in the center of the dresser, between her other treasures.

A deep red velvet couch with matching oversized arm chairs were her choice for the living room and you might think it was too much furniture for such a small room but it was cozy and inviting. On the occasions that brought us all together, we were very comfortable in the space that we filled. It gives truth to the old Irish blessing, "May your house be too small to hold all your friends."

The kitchen was the center of her home and was definitely not to be envied. Everything was old and worn; the floors of both the kitchen and the bathroom sloped just a little but enough that the kitchen floor had a slight incline that would be painfully obvious when walking to the stove. I would not be surprised if the bath water was an inch higher on one side of the tub than the other.

The cupboard was interesting; it had been built into the wall with glass doors that displayed her glasses and dishes. The antique porcelain sink sat on tall exposed legs that were draped with a colorful skirt and in the corner of the room was a small metal table with a porcelain top and four matching wood chairs.

Some might find Grandma Theresa's' kitchen, charming, or nostalgic, suitable for *Country Living*. It could be featured as the quaint bungalow on the beach, very charming, but it was not Grandma's dream kitchen. It was not a place to cook for a family of five. She told me once that she was so tired of cooking, adding that it was just too much of an effort to even put on the tea kettle. It was probably walking uphill to the stove all those years that wore her down.

Her dining room was my favorite room. It was a long and narrow room in the back of the house and looked out over the canal. The numerous windows in this room were draped with white lace curtains which brought in the morning sunshine that filtered through the lace. The table and chairs had a regal stature resembling furniture from the court of Henry VIII. The large dark ornate wood table was complemented by six large, high back chairs. The seats and the back of the chairs were covered with a brown velvet upholstery and lent the room a formal elegance.

There was also an interesting antique buffet, where she proudly displayed her favorite china and crystal serving pieces.

I remember only one Christmas when the family celebrated Christmas day around her table. I was only three years old and it was just a quick glance for me at the dining room and a hurried merry Christmas. They were all having such a great time, a very festive holiday, all except Marguerite, who had the misfortune to have a high fever on Christmas day. I gave a quick long-distance wave and then I was quarantined into Pop's bed for the remainder of a not very memorable Christmas.

This Labor Day, my Grandma served some chips and pretzels and Pop took out some extra chairs. They were filled in a short time and then to my mother's joy we would need one more chair; Bud had arrived to join the party.

Uncle Marty, Aunt Peggy, and my cousin Nancy lived next door to Grandma and Pop and the two connecting back porches made for a generous space for our family parties.

It began this way and every Fourth of July and Labor Day that followed, the party grew in numbers and refreshments. Pop would decorate his back porch with lights shaped to resemble Oriental lanterns, and flags would fly from the front and back of his house. As the years passed, families would turn to the men and their barbecues to cook hamburgers and hot dogs while clever wives would encourage them with praise for their culinary skills. Every family would bring a salad but my mother brought her famous baked beans and when the meal was over, the cousins gathered around the grill to toast marshmallows.

If it is the Fourth of July, fireworks and sparklers begin to surface and, under a dedicated supervisor, the sparklers are handed to any of us who are brave enough to hold one.

I lean out over the fence and similar parties are repeated across the canal and down the street. The tide is high and a few boys are swimming from a small boat. They are having a great time and I wished I could join them.

Eventually, all the fireworks have been set off and when quiet replaces the "oohs" and "ahs," Uncle Marty, after a few too many beers and a motivation to entertain the group, goes into the house and returns with his police department gun. One more round of noise and fire. He shoots his gun into the air above him and it returns down to earth and puts a large hole in his boat. The finale of the evening is watching his boat sink. That will be hard to top next year.

Chapter

19

In 1920, there were twenty-five full-time families living on the island. My grandparents were two of these nautical pioneers.

For many years, the only island inhabitants were birds, insects, and small wildlife but in just a few short years a new town was emerging.

A large well was dug and Broad Channel now had water. There were many times when my homeland had more water than they would have liked but it was not the kind you can drink. Eventually, electricity was available but then only on a limited basis. At the end of the allocated cycle, a horn would blast as a warning that the electricity would soon be shutting down. As exciting as it might have been to live on an island, it also had to be a challenge to homestead here.

I think about my grandmother Theresa and wonder if she really wanted to leave her friends and neighbors in her beloved Manhattan to move to an undeveloped island. Did she worry about her children and their education? Was she ready for the challenge to raise her family in a little house, surrounded by sand and water, in a town that provided very few necessities?

My mother was only eight years old when they moved and surely that was better than leaving her friends as a teenager but we know that any age is difficult to leave your school and friends. Her new life would bring her to a school in the close-knit community of Rockaway Beach, where families had been friends for years.

At the end of the day, did Theresa walk down through the thick sand to the end of the road to look across the bay at the skyline of the city she loved and could only dream about returning home?

Pop was a loud and imposing figure. He was the first voice you heard when entering a room and he was the last voice you heard when leaving. He could be very charming, always loud and enthusiastic, and as loud in his anger as he was in his charm.

It was probably Pop who made the decision for both of them. I can see him wearing Grandma Theresa down with his dream, working on her soft side until she agreed to join him in his dream for a new life.

He was working in construction, going from job to job, and he knew the demanding work would ultimately take its toll on his body, and he now saw a future in this new town.

The town was growing and he saw the many opportunities that would soon be opening up and he wanted to be the first on line when it happened. He also had his dream of spending his days on the bay as his own boss—an entrepreneur, not bad for the Irish boy from Buffalo. He knew they would be happy there.

Summer in Broad Channel is the breeze that soared across the ocean and skims the white caps of the bay surrounding our house until it moves the curtains of my bedroom on a hot summer night. It is the music of the water lapping against the bulkhead with a rhythm that finally lulls me to a gentle sleep.

For me, it is watching my mother swim, graceful and strong, her colorful bathing cap helping me to track her progress. It is the crimson setting sun as we dip the oars of our small boat through the waters of the narrow corridors of the marshy land known as the cow path. It is all these things and more.

My grandmother was aware of the beauty surrounding her new home but she also knew the reality of her new life and the obstacles that faced her.

Grocery shopping with small children would require dragging a wagon through the sand for several difficult blocks, knowing it would be even more grueling on the return home. There were boardwalks in the dunes but a strong west wind might cover them with sand before your return trip home.

If you stepped on a nail or a fish hook was wrapped inside your thumb, it would be necessary to take the train to Rockaway in order to see a doctor. If there was an emergency, a caring neighbor might take you across in his boat.

During her first full summer spent in her new home, she might rethink the dream to live on an island. It would be necessary to have enough repellant for serious mosquitoes and be ready for a thick invasion of gnats on a calm evening. A large hat would be helpful to hide your frizzy hair after an abundance of humidity and finally the dreaded hurricane.

If a hurricane is forming in Africa in today's world, the population of the East Coast of the United States will have ample warning to prepare for the dreaded event, but in the 1920s, weather forecasting was a new science. Radiosondes, transmitters in balloons, were introduced as a means of predicting the weather but it had its limits and so did the island's electricity. A little knowledge can be fatal in the path of a hurricane.

Chapter

20

Pop's dream began to evolve and went by the name of the Lumberette. It was a large steam-powered vessel and together they worked to bring to Broad Channel almost all the supplies the new consumers would need. Martin's workplace was now the bay he learned to love.

My grandparents bought two houses in Rockaway and they spent their first two winters in a solid heated house; the other house was a summer rental.

My mother was born in Manhattan in October of 1912. She moved to Broad Channel as a child and I do believe she adapted to her new life very quickly. As the full-time population in Broad Channel grew, so did her social life. Her brother Marty was seven years her junior and Rosemary, the youngest, was born two years later.

Marguerite loved to read, enjoyed poetry, and was an excellent swimmer. She enjoyed the Mardi Gras but she did not enjoy her mother entering her in the parade, dressed in very silly costumes. My mother was never known to be silly; she enjoyed attention but on her own terms.

She never talked at length about her childhood, just little bits and pieces, but one day she told me of the day her father took her lobster fishing in his small boat. If I close my eyes, I am sitting beside her in that little boat. Her hair is blond, cut blunt with short bangs. It is a beautiful summer day and the bay is calm. A small wake follows the boat and my mother's hand is over the side of the boat and she enjoys the cool water splashing over her arm. She and Pop share a sandwich as her neighbors wave to them from the shore.

Pop had a good catch that day and several lobsters are crawling around the bottom of the boat. She giggles and pulls her legs up and under her to protect her feet from the crawling critters. Marguerite and her father look forward to a supper of boiled lobster dipped in butter. My Grandma told me that her family used one pound of butter every day. I remember reading that an Irish family's status was measured by the butter on the table. My mother is happy to spend the day with her dad and to surprise her mother with the catch of the day.

The little house on Eleventh Road is now heated and the Gronachans are full-time island residents. Grandma Theresa, exhausted from the frequent moves, is busy unpacking and settling in. She calls on my mother Marguerite to babysit for her brother, Marty, and babysitting will become a lingering chore for my mother, especially when another baby will follow…her sister, Rosemary.

The beautiful sunsets appear earlier each day and it signals the end of another summer season. After the annual Labor Day Mardi Gras concludes, the time has come for the island children to return to school.

September is a sad time for the boys and girls who live with the bay. Summer always seems to be the shortest season. Fishing poles and killie traps are stored away for the winter and shoes are reluctantly once again part of their wardrobe. It is a bit easier for the girls than the boys. The girls look forward to new school clothes and the excitement of seeing school friends and, for my mother, a new reader, but the boys from the beach are simply depressed.

The student body is very small and even the youngest of them will travel to a Rockaway school. There is talk among the men of the town to build a school house and then, quite suddenly, a small miracle came in with a blast.

The same season that is blessed with beautiful sun-drenched days mixed with a hint of autumn also brings the dreaded hurricanes that threaten Broad Channel. In 1920, one of these notable storms brought the children a lovely little school house and someday it will be known as PS47. It came with an interesting Broad Channel history; this building was once a dance hall that broke away from its foundation and floated down Sixth Road during the hurricane.

The men came with time and tools and, working together, the building was moved and renovated into a two-room school house, complete with a small kitchen. Those who believe in ghostly spirits might conjure up a vision of dancing couples surrounding the children during their lessons and whispering in their ear the solutions to their times tables.

My aunt Tootsie, Rosemary's new name, was a student in the little school house. She remembers how special she felt when she was appointed to lunch duty. With a great sense of importance, she would report to the kitchen and begin her assignment of putting on the tea kettle and serving her classmates hot tea.

My mother did share a story with me of her difficult commute from Broad Channel to the Rockaway school. September had arrived and she was finally free of her brother and was eager to return to school. The distance from her home to the Long Island railroad station was almost a half mile. Every school day she would walk to and from the station with her friends. Winter was brutal and they walked through the freezing rain or snow and always over sand dunes. She probably spent a good part of her day emptying the sand from her shoes and books. It has been said that once you get sand in your shoes, you will never leave. Grandma had her share of sand and never left the island to seek a different home. If she missed the train, her only hope of reaching her school on time was the kindness of a neighbor with a boat or maybe her father's Lumberette.

Along the road that borders the railroad tracks lived several neighbors who would bring hot chocolate to the children who stood waiting in the cold for the train. It reminds me of my walks to school and at a very early age I understood the theory of a wind chill factor.

Chapter

21

The 1920s was a time for healing following World War I and the flu pandemic of 1918. The number of combined deaths from these two horrific events was staggering and the country was sorely in need of a reason to be happy. The roaring '20s and the introduction of the Charleston were the beginning of a new day but that was interrupted by the eighteen amendments that went into effect in 1920. It was to be known as Prohibition.

Prohibition prohibited the manufacture, transportation, and sale of alcohol, and this historic era was introduced to the country as "The Noble Experiment."

The bill was passed by Congress as a result of pressure from temperance groups but it did little to transform the people of the United States into a nation of teetotalers. It did, however, give birth to a new breed of criminals or saviors, depending on which side of the fence you stood.

Speakeasies, clubs where bootlegged alcohol was available became an illegal necessity in 1920 and what better place for bootlegging than a town that was surrounded by miles of water?

The clubs, featuring entertainment and alcohol, were located throughout the island and Pop's Lumberette was responsible for delivering the liquid gold. The careers of many well-known entertainers were launched from these clubs, including those of Mae West and Jimmy Durante.

Good gossip and folk lore will become increasingly interesting as the years pass, and I can only speculate on the legends that tell the story of Pop's career as a bootlegger.

One story begins with the fact that the police knew Pop very well; he was a business man, a voting citizen, and a member of the church. Maybe the police were his neighbors and maybe they looked the other way. But knowing Pop as an old man, it is very easy to believe that Pop in his prime was a legend and these stories could be accepted as truth.

I can picture Pop showing up in court with his head held high and a slight swagger to his walk, to face the judge after being intercepted by the police.

The accused enters the courtroom, looks up at the judge, and gives him an unusual greeting. The judge, of course, recognizes the salute of the Knights of Columbus and dismisses all charges, infuriating and frustrating the arresting officer.

A second story tells of an even more brazen and calculating Martin Gronachan. The police come aboard his boat and identify several large, heavy barrels as illegal alcohol containers. They now have the evidence that they have been waiting for; he will surely go to jail.

Pop is meek and apologetic as he speaks to the police. He pleads, "Okay, you've got me, but let my crew go. They are not involved, they are just kids; I am the one you want."

It went nowhere; the cops refused but Martin persisted, "Think about it: these barrels are very heavy; it is impossible for you to move them without my help. If you agree to release the boys, I will help you transport the barrels. I give you my word. I have a horse and wagon. Take me into town and we will return with the wagon." He convinces them and the boys are told they are free to leave. Pop and the officers set off to get the horse and wagon.

Returning to the boat, they load the barrels onto the wagon. He is brought into court with the barrels and the judge orders them opened and sampled. The alcohol has miraculously turned to water—salt water, in fact.

Pop's face wore the innocence of a child as the judge declared him not guilty. His crew had remained on the boat just long enough to dump the alcohol and fill the barrels with salt water.

Prohibition was a costly mistake: alcohol was always available, just a little harder to find. There was an element that would benefit from the new law and that was organized crime. Al Capone and his "family" controlled the sale of all illegal alcoholic drink.

Used in moderation, red wine is recommended for a healthy heart. It has existed for thousands of years. We read of wine and vineyards in the Bible and throughout history and then, one day, it all changed. On January 21, 1920, you could no longer enjoy the simple pleasure of a glass of wine. The forefathers of our country, after signing of the Declaration of Independence, probably toasted each other with a glass of wine.

This town needed its beer. The roots of Broad Channel were watered by the philosophy of very hard work and a beer when the work day was done.

At the end of the day, Channelites would gather at a club or saloon to talk about the state of the world, catch up on local news, and open a beer. These taverns were not limited to the young or rowdy; there were some rowdy seniors who loved to dance and escape the realities they faced during the day.

A Prohibition raid would only add to the fun. It was a thrill to escape the perhaps less than enthusiastic efforts of the local police. Perpetrators escaped arrest by jumping over the railing and into the bay but stopping first to see if the tide was high.

The following night there would be reminiscing of the excitement of the previous night's raid, complete with the bragging rights of a perfect getaway and mocking the system.

Pop was still a young man and the years had been good to him. He enjoyed the status that came with being captain of his boat. He probably loved the middle-of-the-night runs and, even more, bragging about it the next day.

The children were healthy and my mother was almost a teenager. Life was good. She spent her summer days at the Broad Channel Bathing Park. With her friends, she swam in the pool, perfecting her stroke, and worked on her time. She enjoyed tennis or just hanging out with her friends, maybe a beach party. But she continued to babysit and did not enjoy that at all. Marty was the middle child and loved his older sister but, like all little brothers, he would exhaust her with his teasing.

Before she knew it, Theresa's babies were no longer babies, just two young children and a preteen. So Grandma Theresa's life was getting easier, allowing her some free time. She was a young mother, one hundred years ago, living on a primitive island in the wrath of Broad Channel winters. Pop worked long hours on the boat, sometimes day and night; I am sure she had some lonesome days. Her life required good friends and neighbors, soul mates, raising their children in the midst of monster storms, blowing sand, and high tides.

The ladies formed a social group, the Jolly Fourteen, a group of island ladies who became close friends; the only requirement for membership was a hearty and frequent laugh.

Occasionally, the ladies took a train to the city to shop or take in a show. One day, obviously desperate for a babysitter, Tootsie was left in the care of her father. Pop Gronachan's business had expanded now to the sale and delivery of ice, a very necessary staple in the days before refrigerators. He delivered the ice with his horse and wagon throughout Broad Channel and now he would have the company of his younger daughter. He placed a blanket on a large block of ice and his little girl sat proudly, feeling both very proud and a chill where she sat. I can see his lady neighbors, some laughing, others thinking, *That damn fool, Martin Gronachan.*

Pop was resilient and would adapt to whatever life would deal him. He was in his eighties when he was admitted to Peninsula Hospital, diagnosed with a blood clot in his lung. He was still a strong man, opinionated and very independent. As we approached the hospital, we saw a small crowd pointing up at a window on the third floor.

There was a makeshift clothesline strung across a window with several pieces of men's underwear drying in the wind. We just assumed it was Pop's room and he did not disappoint us. He survived the blood clot and returned home with clean underwear.

Chapter

22

There was a buzz flitting around town. Everyone was talking, over breakfast in the coffee shop, at town meetings, and over a beer, wherever they might be. There were many who felt strongly in favor of it and a very vocal group against it. There were plans on some city official's desk for two bridges to connect the island to the mainland.

The automobile was now an intricate part of transportation and without a bridge or ferry, Broad Channel would not prosper economically or socially.

On the other hand, a bridge would change the charm of their haven and the essence of what these early settlers were seeking when they migrated here. These were individuals who lived to walk to a different drummer.

Their quiet main street would change into a main thoroughfare connecting Manhattan and Brooklyn to the beaches of Rockaway. Of course, the plans for the bridges would become a reality regardless of any opposition, and it changed the town forever.

The islands in the bay were famous for available whisky; it was never much of a secret. Prohibition continued but the "great experiment" never achieved greatness. Pop and his cohorts continued their "rum running" and then one day it was no longer funny but sadly turned tragic. Pop's boat was the target of one of these raids and this time he was not able to talk his way out of it. An agent sunk his boat and during the raid his partner was killed.

I am not sure if Pop left Broad Channel heading to California to flee the police or to avoid facing the family of his slain partner. Perhaps it was because his livelihood was gone, sitting at the bottom of the bay, or maybe he was just plain tired of the cold winters of the Northeast.

Whatever the reason, they were packing up the car with plans to spend a winter in California. Marguerite was again leaving her friends and school, but this time it was when a young girl's happiness is measured by her friends. But then she was going to Hollywood!

My grandma Theresa moved quickly through the house, packing only what she thought was absolutely necessary. I am sure many thoughts were going through her head, maybe Tootsie was making her first communion this spring. Or she must notify the milk man and stop the mail. They have tickets for a fire department dinner. She had plans to see a play with her friends. Would Marty be carsick and would they have a safe journey? It was only the summer of her young life and Theresa's stamina had been already tested many times. There were multiple moves, the endless snow of Buffalo, the winds and isolation of an early Broad Channel, and now she would face the ultimate test.

She would leave the safety and security of her home to sit in a car for a three-thousand-mile trek, surrounded by a loud and demanding husband, who would probably refuse to ask directions, and the impossible task of entertaining three restless children. They would drive through the Mohave Desert without air conditioning through the mountains without heated seats. The tires were flat as often as the kids needed a bathroom and they traveled without GPS or cup holders.

I don't know if Pop was looking over his shoulder for the first thousand miles but, to his relief, there was no chance of getting caught in traffic, just bogged down in dirt or sandy roads that weren't always roads. The further west he traveled, the more often it was necessary to pull over to visually separate the road from the sandy flats.

There would be many tedious, boring miles, when the landscape never changed. They drove though violent storms and searing heat and it seemed that the three who occupied the back seat were always fighting for a window. There would be moments when they wished they never left home and then one day the topography changed. They had reached the mountains. Never in their life had they seen such high and beautiful elevations. After a period of solemn admiration, reality set in and they realized that they now had to climb up, over, and down this massive wall.

Pop, always wearing his macho bravado, would enjoy the attention of the locals noticing his New York license plate and the three Yankee children sitting in the back seat. He might be teased that he was a bit loco but he would just brag that the trip was a piece of cake. The journey would take on a new life with the breathtaking vistas unique to the West. With the first sightings of authentic Western cowboys who were leading the herd and beautiful, wild horses crossing the desert, all traces of homesickness probably vanished.

For the remainder of their trip, the landscape visible from their small car never ceased to amaze them: the beautiful desert with red jagged rocks, cacti, cattle ranches, and the beautiful raging rivers.

And then one morning the air was cooler. They inhaled the familiar fragrance of salt water and they knew they had made it all the way to Los Angeles, the City of Angels. My mother probably kissed the ground getting out of that westbound car for the last time. Los Angeles appeared very beautiful and exciting to her, the future world traveler.

Marguerite was registered at Hollywood High School and she was so proud to be a member of the student body. She loved the campus with the white buildings surrounded by deep red poinsettias. French was her favorite subject and many of her classmates would later become recognized actors. She loved being part of this beautiful city. I think for the rest of her life she would flaunt her ability to say, "I went to Hollywood High."

They found an apartment and it wasn't long before Pop was working on a movie set. He neither sang nor danced but there were times in his past that he could have won an Academy Award for acting.

Pop was hired to move scenery on the sets and there was a time he chauffeured Mr. Charles Chaplin. He certainly would have kept Charlie entertained with his endless Irish fables. They spent the school year in California and when my mother's exams were completed in June, they returned to Broad Channel for the summer. They knew the lay of the land, were veterans of the routine, and the following fall, they set out to do it all over again, heading west to spend another winter in California.

They were now all prisoners of the love of the road. My mother and her sister were seasoned travelers and would never tire of exploring new countries. Marty traveled to many parts of the globe as an officer in the army during World War II. When he returned, it would be many years before he would leave the security of being stateside.

When I was a child, I was always comfortable to be with Pop. He had mellowed in his delivery by the time he was my grandfather. But we all remember him as a loud and energetic man. He moved with an abundance of energy and enthusiasm, approaching every obstacle with confidence. I always knew he was happy to be with his grandchildren; we were a new audience in his life.

When the cousins were together, we each had a Pop story to tell, and we have a few.

Pop kept a small boat and motor in back of his house and when Dad and I were dating, he encouraged us to use the boat. We had a few perfect afternoons swimming off Breezy Point and Pop was pleased with his role as the benefactor. Soon after we were married, we bought a seventeen-foot wood boat with a small cabin and Pop again was generous and offered his dock space to us to keep our boat behind his house.

He never liked that boat. He said it was not seaworthy and, with a growl, he told us it should only be used on a lake. He resembled a drill sergeant, instructing Ted on the proper way to secure a boat to the dock.

This was our first boat but Dad was very familiar and careful with ropes and knots, weather and tides. The next morning we arrived at Grandma Theresa and Pop's house and Pop was being Pop. He was very excited, telling Dad that the boat had broken away during the night and floated up the canal. He continued, telling us how difficult it was for him to get into a boat to rescue our boat. Upon close inspection, Dad saw it was not the boat that left the dock; it was the dock that left with the boat. Pop had salvaged his float and our boat; his ropes just did not hold.

When his Theresa died at eighty-three, Martin put the house up for sale, packed his car, and moved to the Florida Keys. He bought a trailer, some sun screen, and became a conch. This scenario depicts Pop as cold and unfeeling, leaving everything and everyone behind without ever looking back. I never saw Pop cry, not even at Grandma Theresa's funeral, but there is a saying, "Irishman don't cry." Maybe not, but I am sure as he pulled away from the little house on Eleventh Road, his mind was full of images of his Theresa. They were married over sixty years and had been through so much together, good and bad.

Even as Pop aged, he continued to be strong and independent. Whenever an obstacle crossed his path, he managed to go around it, over, or under it and land on his feet.

He was independent, fearless, and of strong character with the emphasis on fearless, except for the time when a large snake was spotted slithering on the fireplace mantle in his upstate New York house. We were preparing to return to the city and Mary was giving the mantle a quick dusting as I straightened up the kitchen. She was the first to see it and Pop was the first to clear the room. He was clever and he was quick to delegate to Dad and Uncle Danny the assignment of removing the reptile. Pop was a happy man when that snake left the house and he could now come back inside the house.

My uncle Marty, Pop's son, was already living in the Keys. He moved to Florida when he and Peggy divorced and the Keys were very conducive to Marty's unconventional behavior. Marty had taken up scuba diving and devised an underwater camera that took some wonderful underwater shots. He wasn't always as stable as he should be but he lived with his demons as best he could. And he was a diversion for Pop and a familiar face when he arrived.

Pop was a minority in the trailer park; he was a single man with a beating heart and a detectable pulse. Very soon he had a group of women friends who were in and out of his trailer with baked goods and invitations to dinner.

He was a handsome man, especially to the ladies with pre-surgical cataracts. He dressed in his white shirt and shorts, a nice contrast to his dark tan, and he was proud of his thick white hair.

The first time we visited him in Florida, we had a first sighting of the senior happy hour and we found it a very interesting vision. I had a view of the North American snow bird. This particular featherless species migrates sometime after the winter solstice, down through the corridors of the Northeast to a warmer climate for the duration of the winter. For the most part, they traveled alone as the male species tend to expire first.

They are a monogamous group, having successfully raised their young and nudged them out of the nest. Their homes have been closed for the winter months and they look forward to days of fun in the sun. They draw strength from the company of the species who are most like themselves: senior in age, young at heart.

The sun is closer to the horizon and the sky is now a brilliant palette of red and gold creating a beautiful silhouette of the rows of palm trees. It is almost sunset and a procession of lovely ladies is heading in the direction of Pop's lanai. It is the early '70s and the ladies are dressed pretty and proper. The attire of the hour is a polyester or cotton pastel sundress that is complemented by white or gray hair. The ladies from the Midwest favor a low-maintenance tight perm but the less conservative women from the East Coast opt for a more natural look. I can hear the chirping as they walk along the path heading to the cocktail party. They carry a Manhattan, martini, or some other light refreshment. If they were motivated, they might prepare an appetizer to share. It is known as the happy hour and for the moment they are happy.

The Broad Channel house has been sold and my mother and Aunt Tootsie clear each room, sorting through sixty years of memories. Grandma Theresa's belongings have been removed but her presence lingers in every room.

My mother's childhood home is no longer charming or quaint but it has crossed over to shabby and neglected.

A beautiful chandelier that once hung in her dining room was found in the attic. It was an oil lamp and now it is covered with dirt and grime. It is a replica of a Tiffany design and although it is missing a glass pane, it remains very beautiful. My mother would like me to have it, knowing it would look just perfect in my dining room.

I agreed with my mother; it would look beautiful in the old farm house but it would be costly to have it repaired. I telephoned Pop to be sure he did not have other plans for the fixture and also offered to pay him for it.

He growled his signature growl, saying to me, "Why would I sell it to you?" I assumed I had made him angry but then he continued, "Whatever I have is yours." He followed it up with, "If you want to make it legal, send me a dollar." I thanked him and told him we missed him and sent him a check, not enough to pay for the light fixture but enough for dinner for two. I saved forever his reply. I recognized his handwriting, and when I opened the envelope, I found my check torn into small pieces and a note in an old man's handwriting that read, "I said one dollar."

His letter reminds me of the traits I admired in my grandfather. I never knew him to be old or lame; he always stood strong and tall in his beliefs, never dependent or needy, and I like to think that there is something of Martin Gronachan's resilience in me, that I have inherited more than just a lamp.

There are days when I am dusting the stained glass fixture and I think of Pop and his last message to me. He was ninety and finally old. His friends were gone and he was lonesome. There is a paragraph in the Anne Tyler novel *Ladder of Years* that had an unforgettable impact on me.

I was reminded of it when Pop died. It reads, "Didn't it happen often, she thought, that parents die exactly at the moment when other people have stopped being thrilled to see you coming? But a parent is always thrilled, always dwells so lovingly on your face as you are speaking."

Pop died in the fall of 1971. Did he think that his family was no longer thrilled to see him coming?

Aunt Tootsie had always been very good to Pop and she was with him as he made a very quiet exit. She and Uncle Jimmy brought him home to New York and a Broad Channel funeral. His death was peaceful and quiet but that was not the case of the day of his funeral.

After the funeral, we returned to my parents' house for food, drink, and commiserating. The tides began to rise and the winds were already howling. It was a nasty storm, even by Broad Channel's standards. From the protection of the windows of Grandma's house, we saw a boat sinking, bulkheads were damaged, and landfill slid to the bottom of the sea. We shook our heads and commented that this was Pop's last laugh; he did not go out with a growl but with a howl.

Chapter

23

I have only happy memories of my grandmother Theresa and they begin when I was either two or three. She was then a healthy, middle-aged woman in her fifties.

I guess I assumed that fifty was old but that was probably because she presented herself as old. She had no physical disabilities, she wasn't arthritic or obese, yet she moved very slowly and with care. I never saw her roll her up sleeves to do the holiday dishes nor did she sit with us to play checkers and I never took a walk with her.

Life with Pop was exciting but not always a good exciting. You had to hold on tight to be along for the ride.

Maybe she would have preferred a quiet, dull, but secure life. His escapades might have just taken the spirit from her or maybe she loved her life but her demeanor said otherwise.

She was short, a bit plump, and not very attractive. She wore her hair, which retained much of its original color, in two braids wrapped around her head so it resembled a crown on Queen Victoria's head.

She was always careful with her appearance and paid special attention to her wardrobe. She had some very pretty dresses, which she complemented with pins or necklaces. I never saw her wear pants and Apple Blossom was her personal scent.

She was soft-spoken with a sweet, musical voice and she was gifted with a contagious, occasionally hearty laugh. She had a very good sense of humor.

Theresa and Pop had contrasting personalities that went like this: Mary and I took a walk to visit our grandmother. Mary had news for our grandparents; she was expecting her fifth baby, Terrance. When hearing the news of the expected blessed event, my grandmother replied very softly, "Oh, God bless you!" Pop, without missing a beat, but I assumed it was with humor, growled, "God help you."

I don't remember Grandma Theresa ever hugging me or giving me a squeeze topped off with a kiss. The Irish, it is said, are not very affectionate or demonstrative and since she was the only grandmother I had, I never expected more than she had to offer. I don't think that I was treated any differently than the other grandchildren.

There was a day when my Grandma was watching me for a few hours. She was very quiet, doing some ironing. I don't know why, maybe I was bored or curious, but I reached over and touched the iron. Without a hug or concern, she walked uphill to the refrigerator to get some butter to apply to my burn. She did ask, "Why did you do that?" and I replied, "I wanted to see if it was hot."

I knew she loved me and I was always very happy to be with her, but Rosanne and I knew we were not her favorites. Michael was the first grandchild and Mary was her favorite. My cousin Nancy lived next door and spent the most time with her. Nancy was a very lovable little girl with her large brown eyes and her mother's wonderful smile. She was able to in and out of grandma's house whenever she needed and that was good for both of them.

Aunt Tootsie and Uncle Jimmy lived about twenty miles from Broad Channel. When the three long-distance cousins visited, it was exciting for everyone. Eileen was the baby cousin and the boys loved to fish from the back of my grandparents' house. They had such an enthusiasm for being at Grandma's, and Rosanne and I could not compete with that but it took us a lifetime to realize it.

Chapter

24

It was 1929, the year of the infamous stock market crash and the birth of the Depression. Financial experts were not certain if the Depression was a result of the crash or if the crash was a result of a depressed economy left unchecked, but whatever the reason it was the worst economic time the country had known. Lifetime savings were lost to either the banks that failed or investments that overnight were worth nothing.

My mother had returned home to Broad Channel, and was now a student at Richmond Hill High School. The days were bleak and the nights were dark but there was a shining light on the horizon for Marguerite, and his name was Edward D'Arcy Clarity. Ed was affectionately known as Bud and he was called Ed only by those who knew him professionally.

My father's parents, Mary and Edward Clarity, raised their family in Richmond Hill. I never knew my paternal grandfather—he died before I was born—and my grandmother died before I celebrated my second birthday. My mother loved her mother-in-law very much and I wished I had the chance to know and love her also.

My memories come to me as frozen images; they do not move but sometimes they do have a voice.

I have just two memories of my grandmother Clarity and the first image is of a visit to her when she was very sick. She was staying at my uncle Jack's house and I was all of nineteen months old. I see an image of myself on the steep stairs, making the climb alone, and then finding the room where she slept. My father's sister, Sister Joseph Brendan, whom I know as Aunt Mary, is sitting beside the bed where my grandmother sleeps. She sits very straight on a hard-back chair. Her floor-length habit drapes around her legs and her rosary is wrapped around her slender fingers. As I approach the bed, my aunt puts a finger to her lips as a signal to me not to wake my grandmother.

Years later, I would repeat this scene to my mother and she confirmed what I had described. She was very surprised that I remembered it with such detail since I was so young when my grandmother died. She also remembered that day very clearly; that was the day she made a promise to my grandmother that she would always take care of my aunt Mary.

Jack was my father's youngest brother and they were very close. Jack was the funny one, always getting himself into innocent trouble. They shared a childhood and they would recall the antics of three young boys with a stern father and a loving Irish Catholic mother.

The legends of the Irish family are handed down from one generation to the next through the talents of a good storyteller. The Clarity brothers kept the family entertained with anecdotes of their childhood. Jack would be the one caught stealing apples as the rest of the boys ran away. My father would embellish the story to the delight of an audience. Even as an adult, Jack would continue to contribute to my father's repertoire.

The following is an account of a young couple with four children attempting to help a lonely, troubled woman. Jack and his wife, my aunt Sally, vacationed at Thompkins, a very special childhood destination. A serendipitous event for anyone who had the good fortunate to visit there since it was located in the very heart of the Catskills mountains. When we first met Violet

Thompkins, she was recently widowed with five children to support. Although she owned a small piece of the Catskill heaven, she was not a woman of means. Included in her sixty acres of land was a lovely old house of the Greek revival design that is very visible in these mountains. Sitting behind but maybe too close to the house was the lavatory — the smelly, scary structure better known as the outhouse.

She had a small dairy farm with twenty-five cows, chicken, pigs, and two work horses. Violet supplemented her small income by taking in boarders who became lifelong friends.

Grandma and Bud had honeymooned in the Catskills and fell in love with the land of Rip Van Winkle. They returned as a family of five and drove from New York City to hamlet and towns, looking for the perfect place for a family vacation.

Whenever they approached an inn or hotel that looked attractive and clean, the proprietor took one look at me, my age, somewhere between one and two years old, and the "no vacancy" sign went up. I don't think I was ever given credit for Violet's successful business. My parents were very happy with the old house without a toilet that sat proudly on top of the mountain.

Marge and Bud spread the news of the family-friendly, inexpensive Catskill location and soon Violet's reservations would exceed her accommodations.

Violet and my mother became very close friends and upon our arrival we always received a warm welcome. From the moment we crossed the Rip Van Winkle Bridge, Rosanne dreaded those wet kisses and I panicked, anticipating the tight hugs. She would squeeze us close to her ample breast and I would wonder how many children were lost in there, never to be seen again.

My father brought life into the old farm house. He was a tall, handsome man and loved to entertain with his funny sense of humor. He teased the girls who served in the dining room with his silly request, his favorite a large brown egg with purple spots. The girls would giggle all the way to the kitchen and one of these girls was named Pauline.

Even as a youngster I sensed that she was lazy and messy. But I did not know she was a whiner. And whine she did, to my aunt Sally and uncle Jack. She was overworked, she was not paid enough, and they were not kind to her. She was very unhappy working for Violet.

Jack and Sally did the unthinkable; they invited Pauline to come home with them to Richmond Hill. Before you could husk an ear of corn, Pauline was in the back of their car with her meager, messy belongings. She moved in with them to a house that had already met the recommended number of occupants but she did find a job in a factory that manufactured hangers. She was not a good house guest and it wasn't long before she was unhappy in her new position. She was also homesick and turned her resentment toward Jack and Sally.

Of course she moved back to the Catskills and that brings to mind that popular phrase, "No good deed goes unpunished." Violet was very angry with my aunt and uncle for interfering with her household and they were no longer welcomed in her home.

Jack's final punishment was yet to come. Bud would show no mercy in his teasing of Jack. He probably did a parody of Pauline crying in self-pity as she ate the Clarity family's lunch and talked long distance on their telephone.

It was my uncle George who was the first to call my father "Bud." He had trouble with the word "brother" and this given name stayed with Bud for a lifetime.

My uncle George was the oldest of the four Clarity siblings and he was also a bit different from the other two brothers. He served in the military during World War II. He was a member of the Greatest Generation, a machinist mate second-class on a LST in the Pacific. This might have contributed to his quiet demeanor, maybe not. He was tall and handsome and the personification of a perfect gentleman. I never saw him silly or funny but he was always quick to laugh at someone else's joke. He was the one to drive a family member home if they had too much to drink at a wedding and it always seemed to be the very moment when they began to serve dinner. When I asked my cousin George what is the one memory you have of your father that always stayed with you, he will always remember that every night before he went to bed, his father would kneel at his bed and say a rosary. He also knew that his father was very generous to charities to the point that he was called down to the IRS every year to prove his generosity. My uncle George was his mother's son, blessed with a deep faith, which he practiced every day. He was married to my aunt Helen and had two children, Kathleen and George.

I loved my cousin Kathleen. She was spoiled by an aunt who had no children of her own and loved to indulge Kathleen in shopping sprees at expensive shops. Kathleen carried the beautiful clothes like a model.

My mother joked to me one day that the Broad Channel Claritys were the Coney Island cousins. I sensed she was right when I stood next to my cousin Kathleen. She was just one year older than I was but she was cool, with a composed and aloof demeanor, letting me know never to hold her hand. After a few minutes of being together, I noticed I was missing a button, I had scuffed my shoes chasing the dog, and my blond curls were out of control. Her hair was perfect and her skin was flawless, except for a small scar on the side of her face where our dog had bit her.

It is one of those moments that will always be an image stored away in my memory. We had a large dog, an Airedale, and we called him Pep. He was eating from his dish, which was kept in a small, confined space off the kitchen. Kathleen always loved dogs. She was a little girl around three years old when she walked in to see Pep and picked up his dish as he was eating. The dog, defending his food, bit Kathleen on her very pretty face. He had never growled or threatened anyone in the past but the confining space and a stranger taking his dish was a bad combination.

I will never forget the screaming of two horrified mothers, my mother and Aunt Helen. Helen was laid on the couch and my mother put an ice bag on her head as my father and Uncle George wrapped Kathleen in a blanket and left for the hospital.

She carried her scar regally and was always beautiful in spite of it. As she grew older, she would be troubled about her looks; perhaps she thought it was all that was important. When she laughed, she had the same wicked Clarity sense of humor but there was a very sad side to her as well. She began to drink and eventually it killed her. I wished I could have been there for her but I doubt she would have accepted my help. It is always a mystery when two children of the same parents are so completely different. Her brother, George, is successful and happy in everything he does in his life.

My father's only sister, my aunt Mary, had the distinction of having three older brothers. My aunt was born at home, very premature and weighing less than barely two pounds, maybe less and not expected to live. It was said that she was wrapped in a blanket and placed in a cigar box on the shelf of a wood stove to keep her warm. Mary was God' special child, a gift to her mother, and it was a miracle that she did survive.

She would never have her brothers' good looks or their sharp wit but she did have a wonderful, loving, childlike innocence. The day she was accepted into the Order of the Sisters of Saint Joseph was the happiest day of her life. She entered the convent as a bride of Jesus, embracing the life she had chosen.

As my grandmother Mary Clarity walked away from the convent that day, leaving her only daughter, she had to be filled with mixed emotions. She was happy for her daughter but she knew that Mary would never be a part of the family as she had been before. The separation had to be a very difficult time for both of them but Mary knew her family was now the Sisters of Saint Joseph.

She entered into a life of penance and sacrifice. Her days would be very structured and regimented; she would need permission for everything she did. She would not be allowed home for Christmas and other holidays; she would celebrate with her new family. Mary loved her parents and brothers but she never looked back; she was proud of the life she was called to. In fact, if Mary was ever guilty of any sin, maybe it would be pride. She was so proud of her order and proud to wear her habit.

After her final vows, her life was full and busy. She now had a college degree and she was teaching in the Brooklyn Catholic schools. She would go on to receive her master's degree.

She was very interested in Photography and her brothers surprised her with a professional camera. Jack and Bud patiently tutored her by phone and she became the photographer for the order. She covered all the special events and did very well with her new responsibilities.

She had frequent visits from the Clarity families and I remember one special visit to Brooklyn; it was my one ride on the Brooklyn trolley. My father was working and my mother thought Mary would enjoy a visit. We walked the mile to the Long Island Railroad station, changing to another train and then the Brooklyn trolley to Mary's convent. I sat looking out on a busy multi-ethnic part of the city that was so very different from Broad Channel.

The convent, which seemed massive, had two very large carved wood doors. We rang the bell and we were met by a small elderly sister who looked even smaller as she stood by those towering doors. She invited us to follow her and we walked slowly down a long hall with several oil paintings of familiar religious scenes that hung on the walls under the high ceilings. We walked past several doors until she chose a room where we would wait for my aunt . She invited us to take a seat and she would let Sister Joseph Brendan know that she had visitors. We sat talking, almost in a whisper, in a formal austere room with tall windows and stiff furniture. There were no books or magazines but then it was a convent.

After a few minutes, Mary would make a Loretta Young entrance, coming through the double doors, the skirt of her habit trailing behind her. She was animated as she circled the room, greeting and kissing each one of us before my mother brought her up to date with all the family news, Shortly after it was time to visit the chapel.

The world outside was bright and busy. From the trolley I had witnessed a typical Sunday afternoon in Brooklyn: the shops, restaurants and streets were crowded with people who seemed to be in a great hurry as they talked over the noise of the traffic. We walked into the chapel and the serenity and peace of this sanctuary was profound.

Rows of flickering candles and soft light bulbs illuminated the chapel for the numerous sisters who came to kneel in solitary prayer and meditation. At that moment I began to understand why Mary was so content with her vocation.

After many years of teaching grade school, she was assigned to Fontbonne Hall, a girls' high school in Brooklyn. It was the early 1970s and the world was changing very quickly. My aunt would no longer receive the respect from her students or their parents that she had come to expect.

From the time she first entered the convent and wore the habit, she received the highest respect from whomever she came in contact with, regardless of their faith. When she boarded a bus, the driver would signal to her to sit, letting her know he would not accept her fare. Men would tip their hat and women would smile and wish Sister a good day.

As the outside world changed, fewer women were entering the convent and in order to keep the schools open, it was necessary to hire lay teachers at salaries the sisters never received. Also, the number of students registering for Catholic schools was down and it was the beginning of Catholic schools closing. It would take many years but the handwriting was on the wall.

The problem student who in the past might have been expelled was now tolerated and Mary was, in reality, the one who was punished.

Neighborhoods were changing and many Catholic families were moving to the suburbs; the habit was shortened and some of the younger nuns would wear the wardrobe of a lay person.

Mary's life was beginning to fall apart. Her structured life, the protection of her order, was yielding and she suffered something of a nervous breakdown and later the beginning of dementia. She was sent back to Brentwood, where she began her religious life. They kept her busy tutoring, taking photographs, and helping out wherever she was needed. She seemed to be happy and secure again.

Mary also had a courageous side before she succumbed to her health problems; she could actually be fearless. My cousin Gregory piloted his small plane and Mary was invited to go along for a ride. Greg made a landing for refueling and when the plane was being serviced, Mary popped up from the back of the plane and greeted the surprised attendant, "Hi, I'm the flying nun."

On one of her visits to Grand Gorge, she did not need a second invitation to ride a neighbor's horse. She never hesitated but managed to gracefully get up in the saddle, keeping her dignity and her shorter habit intact. Babe was a very large horse and thankfully very gentle, and she enjoyed every minute of it.

She entered the order at Brentwood so many years ago and she returned to her family when she was in need of help. They embraced her and were there for her for the rest of her days. Her memory left her a little bit more each day and soon she had difficulty communicating simple thoughts. I made a poster for her with photos and names of each Clarity family member and hung it on her wall to help her to remember all of us.

She declined steadily and on our last visit to the convent, she had slipped into a coma. I cried when I saw Mary without her gentle smile. I have memories of her lovely enthusiasm and I was ashamed of losing patience with her excessive talking. My mother once said, "If Mary's hat was on fire, you would never be able to interrupt to let her know." But she was always so good, concerned about everyone, generous with her prayers, and so very happy to be with us.

I was pleased to have made those visits and that she had someone to cry for her.

Chapter

25

Kathleen Villiers-Tuthill of Dublin is an Irish historian and author. She has given us a passage to my father's Irish heritage, which began in Galway and Connemara.

My father's family arrived in the New York from Roundstone, Galway, with the surname of Cloherty and at that time the name was changed to Clarity.

A scenic ride from Galway takes you to the west coast of Ireland and the beautiful wild terrain of Connemara. The area's most historic figures were the D'Arcy families. The family tree of the family dates back to 1598 but the most interesting member of the family was John D'Arcy. He inherited his land in 1804 from his cousin and he would be known as the founder of the town called Clifden. We have visited Clifden on several occasions and have a strong affinity for this beautiful town.

In the 1800s John Darcy described Connemara "as been inhabited by a rare breed of people, wild people, wild like the mountain whose principal occupation was smuggling. About this time I undertook the difficult task of improving the land and civilizing the people for which purpose I commenced building the town of Clifden."

I do believe I see quite a bit of the Claritys in John D'Arcy's description of the wild people and know where my wild, uncontrolled blond hair originated.

The town of Clifden was successfully developed with a wide main street called Market Street. A beautiful Irish castle set on wide green acres was home to John D'Arcy. It is a lovely town that overlooks the sea and is said to be the part of Ireland that is geographically closest to North America.

John D'Arcy died in 1839 and his heir was his son, Hyacinth. The town of Clifden continued to grow and prosper until 1845, the year of the famine. Potato crops across the Irish fields were devastated by the blight, food shortages turned into a full famine, and thousands of people died of starvation. Hyacinth fought to feed the people of Clifden. He struggled with the authorities in Dublin, pleading for aid to the town. He failed in his efforts and watched what would be the single most horrific time for Clifden.

The other part of the Clifden tribe was the family of John A. D'Arcy of Kingstown Bay. He was a cousin of the castled John D'Arcy. He lived in a one-story building that was situated on D'Arcy Road. He was Catholic and in 1840 married Winifred King. He had poor land and dependent tenants and he worked hard to educate them. He was a caring landlord but in time he was forced to sell his land and move to a small house, where he lived until his death.

His son, John, returned to Clifden after retiring from the Royal Navy and he opened a grocery store and public house on Main Street. He never married and when he died, he left his property to his niece, Mamie Cloherty.

Winifred was John's daughter and she was my great-grandmother. She immigrated to America and married a man named Cloherty said to be from Galway. They had three children, Winifred, Eddie (my grandfather), and Mary, who was called Mamie.

Mamie returned to Ireland at the request of her uncle John. She lived with him and his widowed sister. They lived over the shop and she inherited the house and business when John died. Mamie married Lt. Michael Lavelle. They inherited Echo Point house and sold the business. Mamie was my father's aunt and died in 1945. She had no children. Her nurse during her illness married Lt. Lavelle and their daughter is Kathleen Villiers-Tuthill.

She became a very good friend of our family and we had the pleasure of meeting her and her family during our visit to Dublin. Our family history was taken from her book *Beyond the Twelve Bens*.

Chapter

26

And it came to pass that Marguerite Josephine Gronachan fell in love with the football star of John Adams High School, and Edward D'Arcy returned the love to a girl he called Marge. The fact that she went to Richmond Hill High School, a rival of John Adams, did not seem to interfere with their love connection.

She accepted his ring. She was in love and her life was moving in a wonderful direction. A high school graduate, she had a full-time clerical position at S.H. Kress Discount department store. She was also enrolled at Hunter College in a part-time curriculum.

Kress had a policy of not employing engaged or married women and if you did marry during your employment, your position would be terminated. She did what every woman in love would do; she kept it a secret and left her ring at home. She was hired at the onset of the Depression and was fortunate to have a job.

Most likely there was a secret underground society, a group of women who where betrothed or married. Corky and Grandma worked together and were bridesmaids in each other's wedding. I can imagine many of the girls discussing their wedding plans over lunch or chatting with pride and enthusiasm about their future or current husbands. I find it hard to believe that the supervisors weren't aware of the truth but then maybe they were also married .

It is very odd that a couple who were responsible for the photographs of so many weddings would have no photographs of their own special day. I often wondered if they had eloped. Like everything else, she spoke very little about the day they married, just in small thoughts or simple sentences about her wedding.

However, this much I know is true. They were married on June 18, 1933, at St. Virgilius Church in Broad Channel. The wedding was officiated by her close childhood friend Father Hudson.

I knew that Eleanor Powers was her maid of honor. They were Broad Channel friends forever and of course, Corky was a bridesmaid. My aunt Tootsie, Grandma's sister, was nine years younger, too young to be a bridesmaid but old enough to have vivid memories of the day and she would share them with me long after my mother died.

She told me about the wedding. Although 1933 was a Depression year, the girls in the wedding party wore beautiful dresses with coordinating accessories, the ushers were handsome, dressed in trendy tuxedos, and Grandma and Bud had a wonderful Broad Channel wedding.

The Nuptial Mass was followed by a reception in the Democratic Hall on Shad Creek Road. The hall is a simple structure supported on pilings and is known to sway with a strong west wind, a high strong tide, or an abundance of rowdy dancing. However, in spite of all of the above, some serious partying and dancing continues there today.

Nineteen thirty-three also saw the end of Prohibition. Grandma Theresa and Pop Gronachan were able to give their daughter a lovely wedding that included a hefty supper accompanied with beer and whisky that flowed throughout the night. Possibly Pop missed the thrill of the moonlight nights, guiding his boat through the marsh of the cow path to deliver his precious cargo. However, that time of his life was now over.

The bride and groom were surrounded by close friends and family who were ready to party. Father Hudson began the festivities with a blessing, the best man offered a toast to the bride and groom, and the meal was served. There was not a shy or self-conscious body in the room. Oh, to be a fly on the wall at my parents' party. Bud would introduce his version of *Heart of my Heart*, complete with passionate facial moves and fake tears running down his face. My mother, a beautiful bride, danced and laughed with her new husband. A few dances were saved for her father and brother and a few others who may have had a secret crush on her, possibly even Father Hudson.

Grandma Theresa joined her Jolly Fourteen friends doing their version of the Charleston. Marty would join his friends and Bud's brothers singing a sad Irish ballad.

There is a strong possibility that some of their guests were living through some hard economic times and that day's celebration offered a few hours to escape reality, laugh, and enjoy a good party.

I really don't know what I don't know but I do know the scene that took place when the newlyweds were saying their goodbyes to their guests and making an exit. After the bridal bouquet was thrown, the happy couple left surrounded by a crowd of well-wishers but there were a few who had a different way of wishing the young couple good luck.

It was a Broad Channel tradition to follow the bride and groom as they left the party. Tying toilet paper or tin cans to the back of the bridal car was just too sophomoric for these Irish young men.

Most parties in the channel would not be complete without someone getting thrown overboard. The temptation was just too great and of course it ended with just about everyone landing in the water. It was our ritual of summer.

Grandma and Bud were married in June, warm enough for a swim in the bay, if the tide was high. A group of young men were planning to follow the newlyweds' car, capture the groom, throw him off the closest bridge. Thankfully, a good Samaritan intervened to rescue my father and the newlyweds were able to escape into the sunset.

131

The newlyweds honeymooned in the small Catskill town of Ashokan. I am not really sure of one particular reason my parents fell in love with the beautiful New York mountains. It could have been the happy honeymoon memories but they would always have a special love for the Catskills and they returned whenever they were able.

The summer of 1933 was a special time of their lives. Their first home was a small apartment in Belle Harbor just a short walk from the beach. From her bedroom window, she had a view of her favorite bay, reminding her that she was not far from Broad Channel.

Summers in Rockaway Beach were the best, especially if you were Irish. Every June, a caravan of winter white bodies, as only the Irish are white, crossed through Broad Channel into the Rockaways, their vehicles were piled high with as much as it was possible to carry. There was always a mattress or two tied to the roof, with each passenger holding on to a rope, expecting to keep their cargo from flying from the car and across the highway.

Some came by train to spend a day at the beach and a night at the Irish town bars. Friends would reconnect after a bleak winter as Irish music filled the street until the early hours of the morning.

Rooms were available for the night or the season in large rooming houses with privileges to a community kitchen. You might prefer to rent a cottage in the miniature communities referred to as courts. These courts were a group of bungalows with a common outdoor area. Mothers would sit with their babies and toddlers, children would play together, and older folks renewed the friendships that were formed many summers ago.

On Memorial Day, the concessions opened and you could have a quick lunch a short distance from the ocean before you headed to the beach. It all came to an end on Labor Day weekend and then the noisy streets became a very cold ghost town.

My parents' apartment was the center of their summer fun but when the weather turned winter cold, so did their little home.

My mother did talk of how cold she was in her Belle Harbor apartment and how she wore her fur coat to bed in order to keep warm. Her dislike of the cold was not a secret, especially as she grew old, and I felt so bad for her getting into bed in such a cold room.

Now, looking back, I look at it differently; she was happily married and wore a fur coat during the Depression—not too shabby.

Chapter

27

Although I never saw photographs of their wedding day, I finally did get to see her bridal gown.

On a boring, rainy Saturday afternoon, my mother brought us upstairs to the bedroom where her cedar chest was kept.. Her mission was to show us her buried treasure. It was a dismal day with strong winds that were accompanied by heavy rain pelting against the windows. However, we no longer noticed. The sisters felt cozy and warm as we sat Indian style on the floor of Mary's bedroom. It was a special time for mother and daughters as Grandma opened the top door of her hope chest. The pleasing fragrance of cedar with silks and satins filled the room as she took her time removing the contents. They were remnants of a life not so many years ago.

A white silk baby book, fastened with a blue satin ribbon, was the first treasure to appear. The ribbon was wrinkled and the silk cover had lost its luster but when she told me it was my baby book, I felt very special. She handed me the book and a sense of notoriety came over me, a book that was all about me.

I solemnly opened the book, carefully turning the pages, and begun to read about the first days of my life.

Page one: the most noteworthy page — a line to write the new baby's full name. My name has many letters so it required some planning ahead. Listed on the next line are the names of the parents and godparents. As I already knew these names, all four of them, I went on to the next page.

I also knew my birthday, that was the very important day that followed Christmas, and now I would finally know the time of day that I entered the world, the day of the week, and of course my weight and finally the location of the blessed event, Rockaway Beach Hospital.

It did not take much time at all to complete my first year. My first smile and tooth (both very early!) were dutifully entered but when I turned to three months, nothing. She obviously grew bored with my progress and abandoned the project.

The seeds of the middle-child syndrome were beginning to germinate. I would imagine that Michael, the only son and the first child, had three volumes scripted in calligraphy to report his first year, stored safely away in a temperature-controlled room.

Grandma continued to proceed to remove layers of lovely fabrics that represented the layers of her life.

She opened a small package wrapped with aged tissue paper that protected tiny, soft baby clothes. I let go of my sulking as she passed them around for a closer look. My maternal instinct ignited. Rosanne and I had a suitcase filled with our collection of doll clothes but this was the real thing. I would always question why these particular infant sweaters and hats were chosen to be placed with her other memories. Were they worn by her first-born or were they waiting for a baby she had lost? If they had some special significance, she did not say.

The next items to come out of the cedar chest were satin and lace. I had every intention of becoming a mother some day and now I knew I also wanted to be a bride, but not sure of what order.

There were two beautiful wedding dresses shown to us that day and delicate lace veils. I was as ecstatic as a six-year-old could be. My mother's dress was very beautiful but I preferred Grandma Clarity's dress. Her dress told me something about the grandmother I never knew; she was tall and thin when she married my grandfather. Her dress was narrow, adorned with many satin buttons, and featured long sleeves and a high neckline. I thought at that moment, *This is the dress I want to wear the day that I get married.*

Chapter

28

My grandfather was the first Edward Clarity and he held a prestigious position with Barbar Steamships, a successful line in the 1930s that took adventurous passengers to exotic parts of the world. It was probably due to his father's prominent position with Barbar that my father found work as a longshoreman on the docks of New York City.

I never met my grandfather but as gregarious as Pop Gronachan was, my grandfather Clarity was serious. There was a photograph of him that I remember very well. He was seated at a desk in his office. He was a handsome man, well-dressed, but looking very grave and stern. It took a stretch of an imagination to see a wide smile on this man's face.

My grandmother, Mary Dougherty Clarity, was a kind and wonderful lady, full of life and good humor, so I've been told. She died before I had a chance to love her; I wish I had known my father's mother.

I know she loved to laugh and was generous to a fault. I stare at her photos in an attempt to know her. I look at her frozen in time, dressed pretty, smiling with love and kindness.

There were times, however, that this middle child, in the hub of a frenzied family, would need reassurance and I would pout to my mother that my father did not like me. She would comfort me, chatting as she made a bed, that I was probably my father's favorite. She explained that I reminded him of his mother and that I looked just like her.

She gave me the license to feel very much superior to my siblings and I beamed with honor until the day I stared at a framed photograph of my grandmother hanging on the wall. It is not an exaggeration to say that I was disappointed.

I was looking at what was said to be a reflection of my own image. The face I was being compared to was a seventy-year-old white-haired woman with a weak chin. My mother always told her daughters that we were pretty and of course we believed her. My grandmother had a kind face with a lovely smile but I refused to see any resemblance.

Chapter

29

L ife was normal happiness for the newlyweds and then on May 1, 1936, they became parents, welcoming my brother, Michael, into the world.

My mother had a favorite phrase as she made pancakes on a Sunday morning when they failed to live up to her expectations: "First pancakes should be thrown out, just like the first child." We all knew she was just being funny and teasing Michael, her pride and joy.

I wasn't a witness to her joy but I know the birth of their baby brought them great excitement. Michael came into the world with the distinction of being the first child, the only son, the first nephew, and the first grandchild to two sets of grandparents.

A new member of the family, and Marguerite and Bud were ready for a larger home. To her joy, the house on Fifteen Road was for sale. It was love at first view and Grandma knew this house had to be hers. My parents were a bit shy of the down payment and her father was ready to help them out with a loan. When I asked her one day about buying the house, she remembered walking Pop through the house they wanted so much and she mentioned to him that she did not know if they would be able to afford the mortgage. Pop answered in his normal gruff voice, "I don't know how you would afford not to." A clever move on his part. My mom was happy with her new house and Grandma Theresa would have her daughter just a short walk away. My parents would never move again.

Three years later, my sister, Mary Theresa, arrived and now Marge and Bud were the parents of a perfect family, a girl and a boy.

It all seemed perfect but there was a dark cloud hovering above and it was not very far from their secure family. The evil went by the names of Nazi and fascist.

The Nazi party was waging war throughout Europe; Japan was brutalizing China and elevated the danger to the Allies when they signed a pact with Germany and Italy in 1941, calling it the Three-Party Pact.

The date was December 7 when my uncle Marty burst into my parents' house with the dreadful news that Japan had bombed Pearl Harbor. My family was enjoying a quiet family day when the world changed.

World War I had been called the war to end all wars but they were wrong; the casualties of World War II were somewhere between sixty and eighty million lives, the highest of any war to date.

The attacks of 9/11 on the World Trade Center and the other tragic targets enable our generation to understand the anger, frustration, and outrage that resulted from the Pearl Harbor attack.

However, there was a very real difference in 1941: young men from every state across the country enlisted and ten million were drafted into the military and shipped to battlefields around the world. Between four and five hundred thousand families who said goodbye to a loved one would receive a telegram conveying the regrets of the government that the loved one was killed or missing in action and a thank you for their service.

Uncle Marty and most of the young men from Broad Channel immediately enlisted and Marty was sent to Fort Dix for basic training. He would earn the rank of sergeant-T, which identified him as a technician, trained to operate and repair tanks.

Sgt. Martin Gronachan, my uncle, was with the 1st Armored Division, which was often called "Old Ironsides," and went through campaigns in Africa before coming to Italy. Marty witnessed the death of many of his buddies, as thousands of soldiers on either side were killed on the Italian beaches. I don't think

Marty ever really left that beach. Marty would talk of a few memories of his life in Anzio. He talked of killing a German soldier in a fierce battle and when the shooting stopped, he went to see the man he had just killed. But it was not a man—just a boy who was clutching his rosary. Thousands of stories can be told with the same message: war is hell.

My grandfather, the other Martin Gronachan, had his own stories to tell. Pop and his buddy Walter Stillwaggon had heard that the army was looking for volunteers capable of running large ships and if they were accepted, they would become members of the Army Transport Corp.

The two good friends and neighbors signed up and were shipped to Australia and it was there that Pop learned that a license was required. He was facing the disgrace of returning home a failure when he heard that the Coast Guard was scheduling a test in thirty days. Passing this test would earn him his license.

Although he never finished high school, he did own a business, in fact a few, some legal and some not, but both improved his math skills. He must call on his ever-present resilience to approach his dilemma.

He was alone, very far from home, and the world was at war. He knew that his only hope of getting his license was to find someone knowledgeable in the study of navigation who would agree to teach him in an impossibly short time what he was required to know. He met an elderly Australian sailor and, under his tutelage, he diligently studied math, including trigonometry, and he became proficient in logarithms, the ability to solve navigation problems. At the end of what had to be a very stressful, exhausting month, he was prepared. He passed the test, qualified for a license, and he earned the rank of army troop ship third mate, serving his country on ships in the China Sea.

Pop served one year in the area of the Pacific Islands and returned home to Broad Channel; the following March, he was reassigned to the Atlantic area.

After arriving in France, Pop had a three-day leave and decided to take a flight to Italy with hopes of finding his son,

Marty. He landed in Italy and hitchhiked north with an MP, making wrong turns but finally arriving at the 68th.

My grandfather created quite a stir when he announced he was Sgt. Gronachan's father. Work stopped, crowds gathered, and Pop was surrounded by soldiers who wanted to talk to him. He would answer endless questions about life in the States. They placed a call to Marty and he answered, "Who's there?" His father replied, "Your old man." Marty was speechless for the first time in his young life.

Marty was given four days off with a car, and father and son did some sightseeing, stopping off at Marty's camp. The neighboring farmers brought roasted chicken and the makings of a great lunch. It was a very special occasion.

The attacks of 9/11 ignited a new war, different from any war the United States had ever fought.

We are reminded that we are at war with the reports of casualties first in Iraq and then in Afghanistan. Every time we remove our shoes or endure a pat-down before boarding a plane, we know why, yet for the most part, our life remains unchanged.

Restaurants are filled, shops are busy, and we go about our everyday life without being asked to contribute to the war effort, although there are many who do so voluntarily.

Every citizen made small sacrifices during World War II, some by choice and for others it was mandatory. Gas and certain foods were rationed and available with food stamps. Women filled jobs that men left when they went to war or they enlisted as nurses, WAVES, or WACS. The women not able to do heavy work knitted socks and hats for the boys.

Rationing was routine and my brother, Michael, recalls the day he almost started a riot in his classroom when he made an announcement that bubble gum was being sold in the corner store. Newspaper and aluminum were recycled. After cooking meat, the fat was saved and returned to the store to be recycled and used for manufacturing bullets.

Chapter

30

My sister, Rosanne, was born to the sound of great rejoicing and celebration. She always loved a good party and decided that this was a good time to make her entrance. But although we were happy to meet her, the noise was actually a reaction to the end of World War II. She was born on August 14, 1945, VJ day. My mother was ecstatic with the news but she was also worried about her new baby. The nurses were celebrating and partying, and probably opening many bottles of Champagne.

My grandfather and Uncle Marty returned unharmed to Broad Channel and Marty married his sweetheart, Peggy O'Gara. She had waited and prayed for his safe return. If Marty had scars, they were emotional and not visible to the average eye. He would always carry those nightmares with him. He never had the opportunity for post-traumatic syndrome therapy and he and Peggy lived with some difficult years.

He joined the New York City Police Department and earned the rank of detective, and somewhere in between he took up scuba diving.

On March 1, 1962, an American Airlines 707 left Idlewild Airport and five minutes later the plane plunged into Jamaica

Bay at the northwest boarder of Broad Channel. It crashed into an area called Pumpkin Patch, just one minute flying time from our house. Marty raced to the scene and volunteered to dive for bodies. It was a brave and noble thing to do but it also added to his nightmares. He began to drink; he was always wired with many mood swings.

Marty's wife, my aunt Peggy, was a vivacious, petite woman with sparkling eyes. If she was stressed or unhappy, she never showed it. She was warm and loving to her nieces and nephews, told a great ghost story, and gave a wonderful back rub. She would leave the adults at a Fourth of July party to join the children sitting on our fence. We were waiting for the fireworks to begin and when they did and lit up the sky across the bay, she was clapping as hard as any of us.

They lived next door to my grandparents and a very favorite time for my grandma Theresa was the late afternoon when Peggy would come over for a chat.

I can see her now, slim and bubbly, sitting on the couch across from my grandmother, holding her cigarette in such a way as to emphasize a thought, her eyes teasing, letting the listener know that good gossip was about to be revealed. She would tantalize her audience, taking her time to finish a story, and keep them on the edge of their chair.

Peggy was Broad Channel. She was everything I love about the people of Broad Channel. Peggy and Marty divorced and she remarried. Frank was a quiet, kind gentleman. He was the complete opposite of Marty but I am sure Peggy always carried some love for Marty in her heart.

Years later, Marty would return to Italy; he spoke the language fluently and would return as a tourist, going back to some familiar places. One of these places was Bologna in Northern Italy. He had been in Bologna when Rome was liberated and during the cities' celebrations, he met Mena. They had definitely had feelings for each other but Marty was engaged to Peggy. He returned to her city and to everyone's shocking surprise, they were reunited. She had never married but eventually she and Marty did marry. He spent the remainder of his life with Mena and her family in

Bologna. She appeared to be good for him; maybe she who lived through the same war as he did could understand his moods but she did not tolerate his abusive behavior. Marty became active in the church and was a popular American accepted by the native Italians.

Chapter

31

There were no plans for my father to go on to college; he went to work as a longshoreman soon after his high school graduation. It was not an easy way to earn a living; it required a good deal of stamina and a strong back but it was a paycheck during the Depression. When the war began, the men who worked on the docks were exempt from the draft. It was essential to the war effort to keep cargo moving in and out of New York ports.

The war was finally over in 1945; the world had endured four dreadful years. It had witnessed the worst of men and the best of humanity. Boys returned as men, ready to marry, start a family and resume their lives. The veterans did have some help from the government in the form of GI loans for education and housing. The economy was good, getting better every year.

My mother gave Bud a brownie camera for Christmas and I am sure neither of them would have dreamed how it would change their lives forever.

I always called him Bud. I never heard him called by any other name. My brother and sister never called him Dad, my cousins did not call him Uncle Ed (it sounds strange to even say it), and my gang of small friends on Fifteenth Road never called him Mr. Clarity; he was just Bud Clarity to everyone.

He had a talent and it was no longer dormant; it became obvious with each roll he processed that he was destined to pursue his art. He studied the photographs of the masters and soon replaced his camera with a professional speed graphic.

His new large camera required oversized flash bulbs, which lit up our childhood every time we turned around. He had three captive models and soon he had a fourth, Rosanne, who one day would prove to be an interesting subject.

He taught himself the science of photography and set up a small darkroom in a corner of the house. I spent many happy hours in the dark room, sitting next to him on a high stool as I watched the amazing transformation; a sheet of paper submerged into a tray of strong chemicals developed into an image that ultimately was staring at me.

It was a strange process how childhood memories materialize. I began to associate memories with a particular scent. When I was a bit older and used a dark room for my own photographs, the smell of hypo, a chemical used in the dark room, brought me back to a time when I was Bud's assistant in the dark room; it was a nice memory.

It was not really large enough to be called a room; it was more like a large closet. But with some planning he managed to have everything he needed at his reach and still have room for my chair.

The Omega enlarger sat in one corner; the chemicals and other supplies were on the counter in front of us. Of course there was the red safe light, , that hung above our heads. Photographs hung on every wall and I never tired of looking at them. I don't know why he chose those pictures but I remember most of them. My favorites were the photographs that were taken in a hospital nursery. Newborn infants were held by a nurse and I thought those nurses had the very best job. For many years, I wanted to be a nurse thanks to these images and Cherry Ames.

There was no running water in the dark room and it was necessary for a quick run to the bathtub to finalize the printing.

The running cold water washed his prints, flushing the chemicals down the drain. His high school football experience helped to accelerated his run through the interference of toddlers, kittens, my mother at the stove, and a large dog, all in a not very large kitchen.

After the prints were washed, he placed them face up on their bed to dry. I would follow him around the bedroom looking at the smiling faces of the wedding party I had met just the day before.

When the war was over, the returning heroes of Broad Channel married their sweethearts, launching Bud's career as a wedding photographer.

Our living room was his studio and almost every weekend, another bridal party would bring their joy into our home. There were no bridezillas in 1945; the young women were thrilled to have their men home and were overjoyed on the day they were to begin their life together.

White satin, lace, and flowing veils float around our living room. There are beautiful shades of taffeta in multiple layers and the occasional hoop made it impossible to sit down.

The perfume of their floral bouquets fills the house and I remember one brave bride who sat me on her lap and gave me a flower from her bouquet.

I am not quite three but I am there. I remember their delight as these ten or twelve beautiful young people pose for their formals, giggling together, relieved that the ceremony is finally over.

Their laughter reaches a new decibel when the bride announces she needs the toilet. Our bathroom was not fit for a bride's dress with expanding layers. Her bridesmaids try to maneuver her train into the small space and the bride is laughing so hard, she cannot speak; all her efforts were to control why she came into the bathroom in the first place.

There was one wedding tragedy that was so traumatizing that I had dreamlike images of a night when I was eighteen months old. I carried these images tucked away in a child's memory until a day when I was older and I asked my mother about that night. I remember our family in the car; it was late and very dark.

I believe I remember that night because I sensed the tension and was experiancing something unusual. I repeated the scene to my mother and asked her about the night we went to my grandmother's house in Richmond Hill. I can see my grandmother coming out of her house and asking my mother if she remembered the butter; I assume she was planning for us to stay for breakfast. It was 1945; I still have the copy of the issue of *Life* magazine and the photos of that dreadful day.

Word of Bud's talent as a photographer had reached Brooklyn and a young couple booked him to create the memories of their special day.

The prenuptial photographs were taken at the bride's house. There were pictures of the bride powdering her nose , another of her pinning a corsage on her mother as her proud father looked on. My father was included in her circle of happiness. The bridesmaids were fussing over her, her mother shed some happy tears, and as they left for the church, the bride and my father were friends.

Bud went to the front of the church, the best place to get the photographs of the bridal party approaching up the aisle from the back of the church. He was surrounded by the bride's family and friends as they waited for the procession to begin. Finally the organist began to play and the bridesmaids were almost at the altar. Everything was going as planned and then, to the horror of her family and guests, the bride collapsed and fell into my father's arms. He assumed that she fainted and he carried her out of the church to give her some air. He placed her on the top step of the church expecting her to come around. An ambulance arrived but sadly there was nothing that could be done for her; she was dead.

Bud's sense of news motivated him to pick up his camera and record the tragedy. The *Daily News* used the photos, as did *Life* and *Look* magazines.

The trauma did not end at the church. Her family would suffer for a lifetime and the stress of the day followed my family for a long time.

The groom, who never would become her husband, saw there was money to be made from the photographs and began to make threatening phone calls to our house. He spoke to my mother and specifically threatened her children unless he received the negatives. That is why we left our house for the safety of my grandmother's house in the middle of the night.

The day my father gave his notice to the dock foreman had to be a test of nerves. To leave a secure job and weekly paycheck when we were now a family of six plus pets was scary but he was ready to leave the docks and build his career.

He was determined to have photography shape their life and when you want something as much as he did, you will succeed.

He began his professional news photography career freelancing for a small Long Island newspaper. He would cover about ten assignments a day and while it was a great learning experience, his eyes were across the bay toward Manhattan and the prestigious giants of the newspaper business.

My mother never worked outside the house, literally. She never washed the outside of a window, planted a flower, or swept a sidewalk; it was as though she drew a line in the sand.

However, what lurked inside the house certainly made up for it. She was managing a photography business; she was both secretary and bookkeeper, kept records of supplies, and she made appointments and Bud's lunch.

Every morning my mother would tune in the radio to listen to the dreary and monotone voice of Dr. Carlton Fredricks, the man who made my life miserable, or so it seemed at every mealtime. He was my mother's guru, her nutritional adviser.

She would begin every morning by lining us up for our daily dose of cod liver oil, followed by freshly squeezed orange juice to wash down our vitamin pills. The milkman left our only other beverage at the front door. Colas or other flavored sodas were an illegal substance in my home with the exception of birthday parties, when we mixed it with ice cream.

Waffles made from scratch with separated eggs or Aunt Jemima pancakes were our Sunday morning breakfast and maybe cold cereal on Saturdays but we were fortified with oatmeal or Wheaten each weekday. I don't know which I disliked more.

If my mother was the apostle of nutrition, the pressure cooker was her Bible. I guess you would say she was excessive in her serving of vegetables cooked in the pressure cooker to preserve the vitamins. I do not remember any dollops of béarnaise sauce or sour crème to make it interesting. Our dinners varied among pork, beef, and poultry and I was led to believe that eating anything fried would send us straight to hell.

Not to beat a dead cow, but if we were invited to a cookout with hamburgers and hot dogs on the grill, we would first have to eat a dinner that included steamed vegetables.

If we whined about our meals, her favorite expression would be, "You need your protein." I was never sure what protein was but I was sure it did not contain sugar. I do believe that my sugar deprivation contributed to my chronic problems with my chocoholicism, not to be confused with Catholicism.

Candy was for birthdays and holidays but we always had one desert after dinner. We did get an occasional ice cream from the Good Humor man with the cute white truck and those thick doors that protected an assortment of tantalizing treats.

In addition to cooking for the family, she had years of preparing strained baby food, formula, and sterilizing baby bottles. She had two babies in diapers with no washing machine. She worked very hard!

Chapter

32

B ud felt confident that he had enough photographs to impress an editor and he had an interview with the *Herald Tribune*. It was a discouraging discussion. Without softening the message, the editor told him, "You don't have a prayer of ever working for a New York City newspaper."

My father thought about it for about five minutes and convinced himself that he would try again. He returned again with a collection of what he considered his best work. This time the editor was impressed but he felt that there was just too much politics involved for Bud to ever be hired..

Bud was waiting for the elevator when he noticed a man running down the hall, heading in his direction and it turned out to be the the editor who had just rejected him. Bless the slow elevator, a twist of fate, or my mother's prayers.

Out of breath, he had trouble asking Bud, "How are you with aerial photography?" My father mustered up his courage and replied that this indeed was his specialty as he thought to himself, *What would it be like to be above the clouds?*

It was a huge gamble: if he did not produce photographs that were fit to print, his hopes of newspaper photography were over.

Sitting in a 747 with your seatbelt fastened, your seat in the upright position, and a beverage waiting to be served is very different from hanging out the open door of a small plane. Fastened by a harness, it allows you to lean out of the door while focusing in on your subject. You can only pray that your settings are correct, although you have checked them numerous times, all while holding a very heavy and expensive camera.

As he was completing his assignment, a fire broke out in Staten Island. A warehouse was fully involved and it quickly escalated to destroy trains and docks.

From his vantage point, Bud saw action everywhere as he and the pilot flew over the inferno. He was thrilled with his shots, great quality with the subjects jumping with action.

It was a sleepless night, waiting to see his photographs in a New York City newspaper, but the morning just brought disappointment when he learned that he was preempted by Associated Press. He was very frustrated, especially because of their inferior work.

The editor called him later that morning and told him it was an accident that his photographs were not used or perhaps it was the politics that he had spoken of. Bud never knew but the editor did advise him to send his photographs to *Life* magazine.

That week, *Life* ran a two-page spread of Bud's photographs of the fire and that was the beginning of an amazing professional career. He was going places.

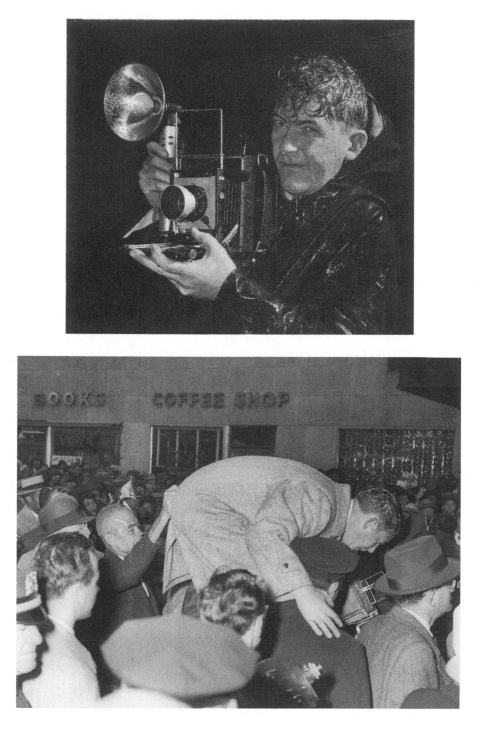

Chapter

33

I have always loved spending time with a book and a favorite story was one of famous Grimm's fairy tales. I cannot remember the title but it was all about a beautiful princess. She lived in a castle and her room was high up in the tower. She had to climb many steep, winding stairs to reach it. She would pass some lonely hours sitting by the window looking out over the sea.

I imagined a bond with the princess; my room was high in our house and, to reach it, I also had to climb narrow, winding stairs. I often looked out my window to see the mood of the bay. There were times when the sea was wild and angry, warning me to stay away, and then there were the days when the water was very calm and peaceful, inviting me to visit.

When I was a toddler, I came down the stairs one morning and I sensed that something was very wrong. The kitchen was different that day; everyone was standing around our dog, Pep, and my mother and brother were crying. Pep had eaten a chicken bone and died during the night. He was buried in the back yard and we all attended the solemn ceremony.

We were not really eccentric but we did have many pets. There was always at least one cat, usually more, and one dog.

The cat population was difficult to control and you never knew when she was going to give birth. We would find kittens in our closet, in the cellar, and, on one memorable occasion, our cat was in labor and ready to deliver in the middle of our paper dolls family. My mother ran in and chased us out of the room; this was not going to be a sex education lesson.

There was very little home schooling done in my family, especially in the subject of sex education. Society in the 1950s was still blissfully prudent when it came to the discussion of sex. Television and advertising were censored and a family could watch a movie or a sitcom together without cringing in embarrassment.

My mother dressed to look feminine and at times a little too sexy. If they were dressed for the opera or leaving for the Stork Club, her dresses usually displayed some cleavage. Her nightgowns and perfumes were a subliminal message to her four children that sex within a marriage was a good thing. But when it came to educating her three daughters, she was extremely shy. I was hanging out in my brother's room one day, probably reading, when a hand pushed through the door with a book. That was it. She had three boy-crazy daughters and she was fortunate we lived by the morals of our faith and culture.

My father was now working for as a newsreel photographer for the paper's television station, WPIX-11, with John Tillman. It was the Christmas season and Bud produced a short film starring yours truly and Rosanne to preview on Christmas Eve.

We were dressed in "company" pajamas, which of course meant that the tops and bottoms matched and there were no visible holes. We shot on location; the neighbors offered their living room as it had the only fireplace on the block. We ignored the fact that one red light bulb replaced the flaming logs.

On cue, Rosanne and I ran giggling down the stairs, holding our red Christmas stockings, and went straight to the fireplace. On command, we laughed and giggled so realistically that even Shirley Temple would have been impressed. The film was shown on Christmas Eve and it was a stunning performance. However, Bud was now promoted to staff photographer; it was the beginning of his career and our finale.

Chapter

34

The first six years of my life centered almost entirely around my sister, Rosanne, and a group of rogue friends on the block. Preschool in 1949 usually meant the hour we spent in the morning getting ready for school and kindergarten was comparable to camp. Our parents released us only when it was mandated by the state of New York. We never had any play dates. Our mothers just opened the doors and out we went to meet with our friends. We instinctively knew to stay away from the water. I don't remember any warning; it was just understood.

Living in Broad Channel, the perimeters of our life were the height of the tides. In spite of that threat, I don't remember any drowning except for one. However, that one single incident was a life lesson with more of an impact than anything my parents could have said.

On a brisk spring morning with a high tide, my best friend, Maureen, and her younger brother, John, were playing with me and Rosanne alongside our house. A six-foot-wide walk that was reinforced with a cement bulkhead was the only thing that separated our house from the wild high tide. That day, John wandered out and slipped, falling into the unforgiving water. I shall never erase the image of John on his back, floating out, his baby face frozen in fear. I stood staring, so filled with terror I was unable to speak. Maureen managed to call for her mother in a quiet cry and plea for help. I don't know if my father heard the splash or Marueen's cry but I saw him running out of the house as he raced to the edge of the water. He started swimming as soon as he hit the water and rescued John.

Our small group of friends was very much the Little Rascals. The little gang was now an assortment of faces and personalities that would grow up in our own special way. I always thought I was Darla but looking at a few of my early photographs, I think I really resembled Spanky.

Who would have believed that Joseph would become Josephine and we would find out that Dennis was such an accomplished swimmer because he had webbed feet? I could accept that Maureen would enter the convent, she was always so good, but it was a huge surprise that Charles would own a successful business picking up poop, placing portable potties around the city. Crazy Jimmy would always be different but Arthur was different in a different way. He would be our first gay friend but at that time gay meant to be happy.

At first Maureen had just one brother but they just kept coming. She lived in a large house with a basement, which was rare in Broad Channel, and there were days when we were permitted to play there. I also spent many winter afternoons playing in her house. Her mother would teach us how to take care of babies, with bottles and feedings. She was preparing us for the future, although Sister Maureen would never have children of her own.

Arthur arrived on Fifteenth Road a few years later. His mother spoke and dressed differently and her house was disturbingly clean. The rooms were sterile with an odor of a mixture of Lysol and Babo. We had to remove our shoes before we were allowed in the house, something I had never done before. We sensed Arthur was different as early as grade school; when he walked, his hips swayed in several different directions.

Crazy Jimmy was mentally challenged but although he answered to what we called him, he was never really teased. He was happy to tag along with us, although he was always on a mission, catching bees in a jar. He lived with his parents and sisters in a house that was as filthy as Arthur's was clean. The odor was so foul that it became a no-fly zone for migrating birds. They were a very strange family even to five-year-olds. His father needed a larger car; these were the days before SUVs. He had two children and a baby so he bought a used hearse, his answer to the station wagon.

My aunt Mary, Sister Joseph Brendan, arrived for her Easter visit and in her kind and innocent nature, she was very upset. She was fingering her beads as she prayed for the tragic family up the street who had another death in their family. Her eyes were filling up remembering that it was only last year when she passed the house with a hearse parked in front of it, but this time it was carrying a crib.

I had a little crush on Charles before I knew what a crush was. Our families were close friends and we were invited to each other's homes. Peggy was very feminine and her lovely house was decorated in soft pastels and floral prints. They also had a full finished basement similar to Maureen's house but that is where the similarity ends.

The basement in Charles's house was more like a night club; there was a large bar with matching barstools, tables with four chairs placed around them, low lighting surrounding a dance floor, and of course the nude prints on every wall. My mother enjoyed a dress that might need a shawl for church but we were a pretty conservative family. Movies were checked in the Tablet's Legion of Decency before we were permitted to see it and the only periodicals in our home was the *Saturday Evening Post* and *Life* magazine if one of Bud's photographs was published.

This was a first introduction to playful nudity for Rosanne and me. There were women sitting on a quarter moon, some wearing sailor hats, and maybe it was tastefully done but my sister and I found it a bit shocking. I did not know where to look but I could not stop looking.

Somewhere in Broad Channel there had to be two very ugly dogs that were responsible for an even more pathetic puppy named Bullets. This dog belonged to Charles and he was slow; he never master even the basic dog tricks and he was boring as well as homely. But he was our mascot and followed the gang wherever we went.

Chapter

35

Bud was now covering all five boroughs of New York City but if it was a slow summer news day, he would improvise and take Rosanne and me to the beach for a "hot weather shot."

This was a very normal part of our everyday life, to have our photograph appear in the *Daily News*, and very often with a stage name. It would not look good to have the subject and the photographer with the same name. It was neither boring or exciting to pose in front of a large crowd; we were just going about our father's business.

As time went on, I began to notice how many people would react to a working photographer. Bud would walk down the hot, sandy beach, dressed in the mandatory attire for a working man: the dress shirt, tie, and suit. His large brown leather camera case was slung across his shoulder and his camera was always ready, in his hand.

Slowly a crowd would form. For some reason everyone wanted to be in the newspaper and I could never understand why. He looked like the Pied Piper, walking along the beach, now with a large crowd following him, hoping to be famous.

Bud had a unique and timely sense of humor and when he wove it into current events, it created many prize-winning pictures.

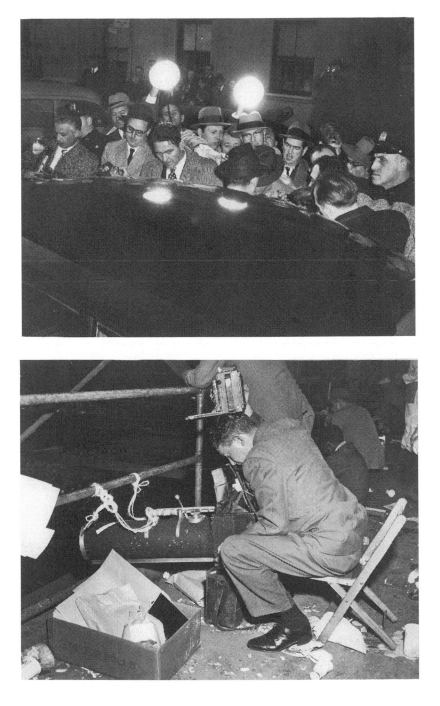

Chapter

36

I read a quote by an elderly Vietnamese woman who described childhood as our lost paradise. My own paradise would last seven years; these were my days of innocence. I was sheltered, protected, and permitted to know only what would shield me from the outside world.

If my parents were sick, I wasn't aware of it. If I was frightened in the middle of the night, I would crawl between my sleeping parents and, without waking, they would make room as though they were expecting me. Occasionally, Bud would tuck us into bed with his wonderful train dance, finishing it off with his "Goodnight, sleep tight, don't let the bedbugs bite" as Rosanne and I, giggling, would pull the covers over our heads as though they would protect us from everything that was bad.

There was the night when I took a long fall down the stairs, landing on my back. My father's loving concern was apparent when he picked me up and carried me to the sofa. A phone call at midnight brought Dr. Werner to our house and while they were waiting for him, my mother and father gathered around me as I lay on the couch. When I began to catch my breath, I sat up and my father whispered, "Marge, she moved." I was actually very surprised they were so upset; it was not the first time I fell down those narrow, winding stairs.

We were insulated and separated from harm and evil by the presence of our parents; they protected us from the truth that would wait patiently for a few more years. The only sorrow I would know during these years was the death of a pet, a gentle push toward the reality yet to come.

We never doubted Santa Claus, the Tooth Fairy, or the Easter Bunny but Santa was the most important childhood fantasy to ever land on our roof. Christmas Eve was the second most exciting day of the year and a very difficult night to fall asleep. After we hung our stockings, Rosanne and I would climb the winding stairs up to our room in the tower and scramble into a bed, taking turns to softly scratch each other's arm, a proven method to help us drift off to sleep. During the night, I woke up startled when I heard the soft ringing of bells. Santa was on the roof! I shook Rosanne and we both sat up with a jolt, listening for the sound of a thump. Eventually, we both fell back to sleep, disappointed after I realized the noise I heard was just the old radiator hissing on the cold winter night and not the bells of Santa Claus's sled.

Sometime between Thanksgiving and Christmas, my parents would take us to Manhattan for our annual visit with Santa Claus. A visit to "the city" was an occasion to dress up and this year Rosanne and I wore ensembles consisting of a navy blue velvet hat, leggings, and coat, all trimmed in white faux fur. The city was at its best during the Christmas season. If you live in New York City, unless it is a class trip or visiting relatives, you rarely visit the tourist attractions. However, between Thanksgiving and Christmas, almost everyone takes the subway into "the city" to see "the tree" or admire the decorated windows of the giant department stores, especially Macy's, Saks, and Lord and Taylor.

We picked the perfect day to visit Santa; there was a winter chill in the air that reminded us that it was December but there was little wind and it was dry and clear. We walked through the crowds of Rockefeller Center and, just like a tourist, I gazed up at the beautiful Christmas tree that towered majestically over the admiring crowd. Dressed with thousands of multiple-colored lights and massive ornaments, the beautiful fir would be the city's celebrity for several weeks, only to be taken down after Christmas, hauled away, and forgotten, never to be famous again.

I leaned over the rail of the skating rink, my eyes glued to the glamorous New Yorkers as they glided around the rink to the sounds of joyful Christmas music. They were dressed so beautifully; the younger skaters wore pompoms on their skates that were color-coordinated to their scarves and hats. The most talented skaters were making their own music scraping the ice as they completed a figure eight or difficult spin. My parents thought it was an apropos time for a Christmas cocktail and we headed toward the rink-side restaurant. The lounge was noisy and crowded but a friendly waitress took the order: two Shirley Temples and two Manhattans. Rosanne and I each had a cherry from a parent's drink and as we chewed on it, we could taste a trace of vermouth and bourbon. We left the lounge and walked through the bustling city streets, the bells of the Salvation Army volunteers ringing on every corner, and the sweet aroma of roasting chestnuts followed us to the door of Macy's.

Taking my place in the revolving door, I had my first glance of the first floor of Macy's as I was rotated into a vision of an enchanted Christmas. It was fantasy land, striking red and gold roping with satin bows that draped around oversized Christmas ornaments and strung from every section of the ceiling. On the cosmetic counters, gifts were wrapped in the same red and gold motif and placed in such a way as to make them irresistible to the passing shoppers.

Finding our way to the wooden steps of the old escalator, we arrived at the second floor and I carefully stepped from the escalator into the seasonal home of Santa Claus. He was presently holding court from his throne and he was surrounded by his many elves. Rosanne and I would join the long queue waiting to see Old St. Nick. We followed the red velvet roping that wound its way around Santa's village and it appeared to have no end. I thought for sure we would wind up on the third floor in ladies' lingerie. It was a bit of an ordeal; the line was moving so slowly, the boy in front of me was crying, and a girl was whining that she needed the bathroom. Finally, we heard the jolly laugh that was highlighted with multiple "ho, ho, hos" and butterflies immediately began to dance around in my stomach. I have never had a problem with shyness, probably the contrary. I may have talked excessively at times, but this was Santa—not his helper but the real thing. Santa and I were now face to face and it was my turn for my three-minute interview. I couldn't mess this up. I took a deep breath and greeted him warmly, wishing him a merry Christmas and reminding him that we met last year, not there in Macy's but at Best & Company. I then began to read my Christmas wish list with some very specific instructions. I am not sure if it was nerves but I developed a twitch in my left eye and he might have thought I was winking at him. I told him goodbye and not to forget me and he mumbled something that sounded like he never would.

Some memories of my childhood almost escape me. My first seven years were secure and happy with the exception of one traumatic event. The day I was discharged from Rockaway Beach Hospital in January of 1944, I had no intention of ever coming back. How would I know when I was just a few days old that Rosanne and I would return one day together to the place of our birth? We had a date with the doctor who helped me to make my entrance into this world, Dr. Werner, to have our tonsils removed. I doubt that there was anything wrong with my tonsils; I think I was scheduled to either keep Rosanne company or then maybe it was cheaper for two sets of tonsils.

It was dreadful; I do not know how I almost forgot to mention that awful morning. I was sitting on a gurney in a dreary hall outside the operating room. As I waited for my turn, a pretty young nurse was entertaining me; together we blew up rubber surgical gloves, checking for holes. Shortly after, I was wheeled into the OR; it was a sunny, narrow room with large windows and, in just minutes, an ether mask, which seemed to come down from the ceiling, was placed over my face.

I was trying so hard to tell them that I could not breathe but no one would listen. I will never forget those circles I saw as I was falling into the deep sleep of anesthesia. When I woke up sometime later, I was without my tonsils and my sister. I just assumed she would be in the bed next to me. The operating room nurse was standing by my bed and she asked me what I was trying to say before I went to sleep. I was both embarrassed and taken aback by her question. I was ashamed of my cowardice and wondering what she thought I was saying: "Please turn on a television. I am missing *Howdy Doody*"? Didn't she know I thought I was dying? It turned out that Rosanne was two beds down and in between us was the site of some horrible, loud noise. It was a boy who never stopped crying, not once during the twenty-four hours we spent in that ward. A little more of that ether would have been a blessing. .

Rosanne had bled excessively and I remember hearing the doctors talking to my mother, referring to her as a bleeder. It was upsetting for me to look at her; her face was packed with gauze and her hands were tied to the bed rail. We did go home soon after, but if she was ever going in for appendicitis, they would have had a hard time finding me.

Chapter

37

Broad Channel might have been the only town in New York City without a park or a playground. There were city politicians who considered the residents of Broad Channel squatters, regardless of the fact that every homeowner paid an annual ground rent to the city and received very little in return. The people who made up our town deserved more. If those elected officials had stood before the honor roll of Broad Channel, they might have thought differently. The World War II memorial stood proudly on the corner of Noel Road and although many of these brave boys who are listed did return home, there were the tragic gold stars that never saw Broad Channel again.

The city fathers should also be impressed with the working men and women of Broad Channel. Many were blue-collar workers and just about everyone worked; welfare was synonymous with failure and an impressive number of Catholics from our town entered the priesthood or the convent. The City of New York was not a compassionate landlord but in spite of their apathy, we were content. Our only playground was the bay outside our windows that beckoned to us and we were happy to respond.

Our daily summer routine followed the tide; if the tide was high at noon, lunch was at eleven, allowing one hour before entering the water. I sometimes question if this abstinence was conceived by a group of weary mothers needing an hour's rest before supervising the swim time. I have never heard of anyone actually dying from eating a peanut butter and jelly sandwich as they entered the water. At high tide we swam and low tide we fished for crabs. We walked around the low water with a crab net, careful not to step on hackle heads or horseshoe crabs that might be hiding under the seaweed or we enjoyed just watching the fiddler crabs on the salt marsh behind our house.

It was 1948, a year in the center of my days of innocence, when my father brought home a large box that held something foreign. The enthusiasm for the contents of this carton was infectious; I was so happy to know we had a television yet I had no idea what it was. This ten-inch black-and-white screen would ultimately change our life forever. However, aside from seeing ourselves on that blockbuster short Christmas film, the television would not dominate our childhood. My mother was vigilant to protect us from the intruder. She was sure it would harm our eyesight or, worse, tarnish our minds. We were allowed a few *Farmer Grey* cartoons, the ones with endless mice coming out the kitchen faucet, and *Howdy Doody*, costarring Buffalo Bob and Clarabell. There were a few other shows that she would scrutinize before she gave her okay. For the most part, it was our imagination that continued to keep us amused.

Chapter

38

We were very fond of our elderly neighbors, the Bradleys, who lived directly across the street from us. Mr. Bradley was a tall, thin, elegant Englishman who boasted a full head of white, silky hair that complemented his long white mustache. Most summer mornings, Mr. Bradley would begin his day smoking his pipe and reading his current book as he sat in his favorite chair that looked out over the bay. Rosanne and I, always friendly, good neighbors, would pay him a visit, chatting away, and if he resented the interruption, he never let on.

Mrs. Bradley was tiny and looked her ninety years but she had the energy of five children and the strength of three men. My mother shared a secret with me, letting me know that Mrs. Bradley wore a wig. I felt very important that she confided in me this weighty secret and I immediately shared it with Rosanne.

The Bradleys did quite a bit of heavy reading, and it was Mrs. Bradley who carried the heavy books, a total of four miles to and from the Rockaway Library. One afternoon Bud saw her walking down our street carrying her hefty load and he did what a gentleman would do: offer to carry her bag. Gasping for breath and limping as he reached her house, he accepted her idea that she carry her books up the flight of stairs and as he walked away, he was sweating, limping, and rubbing his shoulder.

There were two bachelor sons in the large house but she managed the entire household without any help. I enjoyed the visits when I spent time with the Bradleys; our houses shared a common view of the bay but it appeared unique from either house. Their house was large yet cozy but with a strong smell of pipe tobacco. There was one particular room that I found charming, although at that age I would not have recognized the word, just the appeal. It was their small breakfast room in a back corner of the house and was more English than Broad Channel. There was a small table for two that sat in front of the window and if we stayed long enough, she would serve us English biscuits on the table that looked over the canal. An abundance of books filled every space on the book shelves that lined each wall .We did enjoy these visits but especially on our birthdays. Mr. Bradley never forgot us; he would present us with a poem he wrote especially for our special day and wrapped inside the poem was a dollar. The dollar vanished quickly but I saved some of his poems.

128 words.

Henry S. Bradley,
56 15TH Road
Broad Channel,
N.Y.

Where Are You Now?

Where are you now my snow white pet?
So oft I think you linger yet, for on the wall
Your face appears, I hear you call
Me fondly when I enter where
We shared the couch and easy chair.
So well named Mischief just because
You did so much with tiny paws,
Your loyalty, so real, so fine,
Was just a dog's, but part divine
And memory recalled in dreams,
So vivid is, it often seems
The patter of those little feet
Is close behind me on the street,
When, turning round, your paw to shake,
The dream recedes, and I awake
Dear little pal, where'er you be,
There, I belong, just wait and see
When earthly death dispels the fog,
New eyes will see my little dog.

Henry S. Bradley

Chapter

39

I t takes a village to raise a family and my aunt Rosemary was a fundamental part of our village. We called her Tootsie and she was part of the team that kept us in our insulated cocoon.

She was never silly or cool but always a kind mentor with an ardent sense of humor and a keen intelligence. My mother's sister could always be depended on to be consistent and predictable; she was a safe and secure place to be. She would never entertain the family with the stories that her brother, my uncle, divulged. I think Marty's motive was to shock and entertain at the same time. He would always tell a story with excessive animation and boisterous delivery. He and Peggy had a collie. But Marty had come to believe that his collie was really a wolf. He arrived at this conclusion because, according to Marty, a wolf has a different method of drinking water than a dog; they do not lap and his dog did not lap. In my opinion, the wolf looked just like Lassie, a dog.

The story continued: one day my aunt Peggy passed out and fell to the floor. She just lay there not moving. Marty continued but he was starting to lose me. I never heard of anyone passing out and falling to the floor. The dog or whatever it was stood with all four paws over Peggy, growling at Marty, warning him not to come close. Marty told his audience, which included us children, that he punched the dog, knocking him unconscious in order to reach Peggy. I think I was under the bed with my hands over my ears by the time he finished his gruesome story. Aunt Tootsie would never upset children with this appalling, unabridged story.

She was the first woman I knew who drove a car and drive she did. Aunt Tootsie would be both mother and father to my three cousins when my uncle Jimmy was away. He was a tug boat captain and worked a schedule that took him away from home for days at a time. We spent many happy days with our Stillwaggon cousins. Their home in New Hyde Park was our refuge during the hurricanes that might threaten our home. If my parents were going out to a trendy Manhattan night club on New Year's Eve, we celebrated with my aunt Tootsie and our cousins Jimmy, Jackie, and Eileen. One New Year's Eve, we sat huddled together on the couch, watching a very scary movie that we still talk about, *The Old Red Mill*. These were the times of our lives and we have so many memorable days.

Two of these memories will always be with me. One was the day it took three of us to pull my cousin Jimmy out of the clothes hamper. We were playing hide and seek and he found himself wedged in a laundry hamper that was one size too small. The other would have to be the day we initiated the Apple Tree Club. Of course I was president and Jimmy, Jackie, and Rosanne were merely members.

Aunt Sally was another necessary component of our village. Jack and Sally would visit with my parents every other week and I knew it was time for their visit when my mother spent some extra time getting dressed. There was an extra squirt of perfume or a new skirt but the real giveaway was the cheese and crackers on the living room end table. Sally and my mother always looked very feminine and so pretty. My aunt was very easy to be around; she always talked to me as though I was grown up and I will always remember our Christmas visits to their house and her Christmas cookies. As I lay upstairs in bed and listened to their lively conversations followed by loud laughter, I knew how much my parents and my aunt and uncle enjoyed these visits. One morning there was a broken potted plant lying on the kitchen floor. When I asked my mother what happened, she told me it was my just my uncle Jack and my two parents could not contain their laughter. They never explained why no one swept it up.

There were five cousins in my aunt and uncle's house and we would spend a few summer days in each other's home. They lived in Richmond Hill and I finally had a chance to use a city park. I believe it reinforces the family to be surrounded by so many who love us and share our values.

Chapter

40

In September of 1949, I left the sanctuary I called home and entered a world where strangers would determine the mood and joy of my day. I would join the trek of eight grades of students, walking Monday through Friday north to St. Virgilius School. When we arrived at our Noel Road destination, we waited for permission from Dan the Cop to cross the street. His assignment every school day was to protect the children crossing the boulevard and that was probably the extent of protection Broad Channel children would need. He had a warm but serious smile and a gentle, caring manner but he looked like he might enjoy a good stiff drink or two. I joined the chorus of the older children greeting our good friend with the respectful, "Good morning, Dan!"

Sister Estelle was my first teacher and we bonded immediately. She was very kind and had a wonderful, welcoming smile despite the fact that my father brought my dog along to the classroom. This was my first hour of school and I don't know if it was inspiration or desperation but my father wanted an "opening day of school" photo. He decided on a reenactment of "Mary Had a Little Lamb" but instead of a lamb, he was substituting a dog that followed Marguerite to school. This was my first time in a classroom and I would think it was the first time for Curley. If I was inclined to be timid or shy, I never had the opportunity. Before I could even figure out where I should sit, Curley was on my lap and Sister was leaning over us, ready for her close-up. I often think how difficult it would be to replay that scene today, violating all the state and federal laws that would prohibit a dog in the classroom or my father carrying a camera into school without being searched for a weapon, potential law suits, from the parents of children allergic to animals, and protests from PETA.

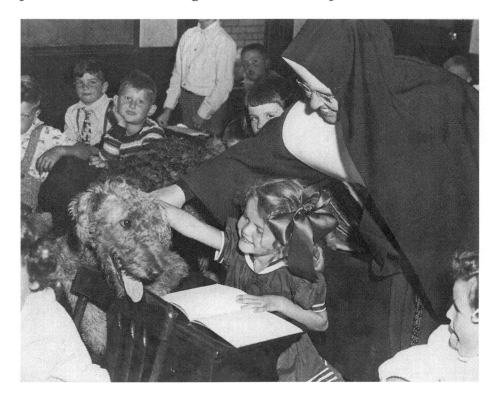

I loved first grade; I was learning to read and it wasn't long before I completed the small primer. I soon had enough of "Run, Spot, run; see Dick run, see Jane run." I was ready for a challenge and anxious to enjoy all that books could offer to me. The final day before summer vacation, Sister gave us some very used second-grade readers to take home and although they smelled musty, I spent wonderful summer days reading that book. Even today, the odor of a musty old book reminds me of those happy summer days exploring the colorful pages of the second-grade reader.

Now that I was a member of the student body of St. Virgilius, I was spending more time with my brother and sister. We walked to school together; Michael was in the eighth grade, Mary probably was in the fifth, and everyone walked along Cross Bay Boulevard in an informal group.

I don't remember anyone arriving at school by car and, if asked, every child in Broad Channel would identify a yellow school bus as the transportation to the summer day camp. Instinctively the older students looked out for the young ones; I don't remember any parents walking with us. There was no cafeteria in the school; the lavatories weren't so great either, so lunch meant that we walked the distance four times a day. We walked on the coldest snowy winter days, we walked in high winds and rain, and only a very high tide would stop us. As we braced ourselves against the grueling elements of a seaside winter, we could hear the screeching laughter of seagulls sitting on the poles above us.

If we should ever need help, if we took a fall or became sick, behind any door we knocked on along the route was someone we knew and who cared about us who would open their door and heart to us.

The innocent days continued during my first two years of grade school. The schoolwork came easily to me; I adjusted well and was happy. We would read stories about Jesus and we learned to know and love Him, learning about His birth, His time here, and His crucifixion. The rituals of the Church were assimilated into our young lives and the structure of our days gave us security.

I have a silent memory frame from that time of my childhood; a night the parish attended a High Mass with benediction. I was one of two winged angels who led a procession of small children. The girls were dressed in lovely white dresses and carried tall gladiolas of the deepest shades into the church. The scent of incense filled the air and candles illuminated the dimly lit church. The choir, accompanied by Mrs. McGovern at the organ, sang "Panis Angelus," and the other familiar Latin hymns used during the Mass. It was the core of our childhood when families, friends, and neighbors gathered together in a very solemn spiritual experience, one of many I would experience as a child. These moments enforced the faith that is a comfort to us throughout our life.

There was an occasional party in our classroom and we always decorated the blackboards and windows for holidays but the last afternoon before Christmas vacation, the entire school, under the supervision of our teachers, walked the mile to the Parish Hall for a Christmas party. When we arrived at the large old dark hall, we were given a box of hard, spicy Christmas candy and were seated on rows of wooden folding chairs. We sat ready and looking forward to a black-and-white movie that was usually a cutesy Shirley Temple film. If we were lucky, the heat was working, the toilets flushed, and the projector did not break down for at least an hour.

Chapter

41

While I was busy with my early childhood education, Bud's career had taken off. His name and photographs were recognized throughout the city; he was "Ed" to the cardinal, the mayor, and governor. Awards that would someday number two hundred were lining the walls of our home.

The peace that followed World War II was a welcomed guest but even before the wounded bodies and minds of thousands of victims were healed, the country was preparing for another confrontation; peace had slipped out the back door.

The Korean War was a spinoff of World War II and was the first conflict of the Cold War. It began in 1950 and the official fighting ended in 1953 with over thirty-six thousand deaths and 8,176 missing in action.

The Cold War was an oxymoron. War can only be described as hot; there are always victims. After the Korean War, which was officially called a police action, the Cold War introduced a very disturbing and frightening new culture. We began to fear the bomb. Books on the subject, fiction and nonfiction, made the best-seller list of the *New York Times*. The president's red telephone and more than two demented foreign leaders sent stress tremors through even the very fearless. We escaped the fear by seeing a movie called *Dr. Strangelove, How I Stopped Worrying and Learned to Love the Bomb*, which was intended to make us laugh, and *On the Beach*, which did scare the hell out of us. Government newsreels were produced with useless information on what to do in the event of a nuclear attack. Bridges had new signage directing us to drive over and exit the bridge in case of an attack and I often wondered what good that would do.

In order to reassure the citizens of the United States and the rest of the Western world, a few handpicked staff members of the *NY Daily News* were invited to visit and report on the United States Air Force bases around the world that could be used as retaliatory takeoff points in the event of an attack.

Two reporters, Joe Martin and Ed O'Neil, and one photographer, Ed Clarity, were selected to cover this significant assignment. The mission would take them around the world as VIPs via military planes, guests of the military.

The tour included SAC bases in Hawaii, Guam, Taiwan, and the Philippines, and eventually would wind up in Europe. Post cards arrived from around the word and contributed very nicely to my stamp collection. Bud also sent gifts from Germany, a large carton of cuckoo clocks for our extended family, and my favorite, a can-can doll from Paris. It was professionally prestigious and exciting for Bud but we on the home front missed him very much, especially my mother. She was lonesome without him; her soul mate was traveling without her, visiting places she would love to see but she made up for it later when she thought that we siblings were old enough to be trusted to be on our own. Never trust four children home alone for more than twenty-four hours.

Bud would photograph many celebrities during his career but this trip would bring him face to face with the most exciting celebrity of his career, Pope Pius XII. His itinerary brought him to Rome and it coincided with the Roman Catholic Holy Year. Bud received a cable at his hotel from his managing editor. New York City had a large Catholic population who read the *Daily News* and the editor wanted a photograph of the pope for the cover of the Easter Sunday edition.

A week passed with multiple phone calls to the Vatican but without the approval for the photograph. The Holy Year had filled the Pope's already busy schedule and Bud's window of opportunity was closing. If he was to be successful in receiving an audience, he would need a few days to get the photograph back to New York City. Finally, while composing a cable to his editor relaying the bad news, the Vatican called and was allowing one photograph, perhaps the next day, but only one photograph.

Bud was admitted to the Vatican palace and was waiting in the corridor under the watchful eye of the Swiss Guard, when he spotted Pope Pius XII entering through the door. He focused his camera and had his shot, the only one permitted. The pope stopped walking momentarily and Bud realized he was waiting for the photographer's mandatory second shots. I believe when I was learning to talk, the first sentence I put together was "Just one more." Without hesitation he took the second shot, satisfied that he had completed his mission.

As he was resting on his laurels, the bells of St. Peter's began to chime and the pope, cardinals, visitors, and Bud knelt for the recital of the Angelus by the pope.

I try to imagine what was going through my father's mind at this time. He was raised as a devout Catholic and he might have been thinking, *If only my mother could be with me now*, or was his thoughts on his sister, who entered the convent? She would be happy for her brother and also wish that she could be with him. But as the photographer, was he just concentrating on his next photograph? Maybe it was all of the above.

As Bud knelt with his camera by his side, he noticed a cardinal making eye contact with him, letting him know it was okay for him to photograph the pope as he prayed. The floodgates opened and Bud took multiple pictures and when the pope completed the Angelus, he approached my father and asked him where he was from and which newspaper he was with. My father explained that the *Daily News* would like a photograph for the Easter Sunday front page. The pope then suggested a formal photograph and he moved toward the throne in an adjoining room, sat down, and posed with a blessing. Bud's last photograph that day was his best and was seen by millions on the front page of the *Daily News* on Easter Sunday.

His conversation with His Holiness lasted over thirty minutes and as it was winding up, and they were saying goodbye, the pope removed two silver religious medals and blessed them and my father's trip home. A few weeks later, Bud had to choose between two flights from Manila to Tokyo and he chose the earlier flight. The other flight hit the side of a mountain, leaving no survivors. Bud would later attribute his good fortune to the blessing of the pope. Quite shaken, he later shared the story with General Douglas MacArthur, who replied, "Ed, you're on borrowed time."

Chapter

42

I believed I was born to lead. I was captain of our street teams, commander of red light- green light, and premier architect of innovative straw forts, and although self-nominated, president for life of the Apple Tree Club. I was unopposed and took office. Someone had to take charge and I was willing to step up to the plate. Rosanne was the sweet, easygoing baby of the family, content to be a team member — that is, until the day she thought she was being ignored and then she turned into a wild, red-haired, angry little girl.

This was, to the horror of our family, demonstrated on the very day Mary was preparing to make her confirmation. Mary looked beautiful, dressed in a beautiful navy blue and pink taffeta dress with a velvet bow. She was holding a large floral bouquet and was seated for her formal photograph and it just pushed Rosanne over the edge.

She approached my father, fists clenched, metal curlers dangling and spinning from her fiery red hair that made her head look like a miniature Sputnik. She was dressed in ripped underwear, since it was my mother's decision to dress her for the church at the very last minute. I don't know if she rehearsed the "face" but, boy, was she good. Bud laughed very hard and turned his weapon of choice, the camera, in her direction, and just kept shooting. It was a blockbuster. The *Daily News* added the caption "Who Stole My Copy of the *Daily News*?" and posted a life-sized advertisement of the famous shot throughout the New York subway system. It was bought by an underwear manufacturer and it ran in ninety-seven newspapers.

It also became a warning to our entire family: somewhere behind that sweet smile and beautiful red hair, a hot temper lies dormant, waiting for the day Rosie Posy is taken for granted.

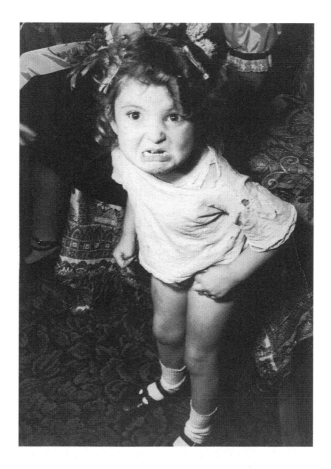

Chapter

43

Publicist — n., one who is retained to manage publicity for another

Good publicity can be a fleeting favor and bad publicity, a shadow that is visible in any light.

Rockaway's Playland was located on 98 Street in Rockaway Beach directly across from the boardwalk that flanks the Atlantic Ocean. It was a destination for summer crowds for many years but today, comparing it to Six Flags, it would be considered a very small amusement park. However, for many years it was the site of many exciting hours of summer entertainment.

It was possibly a photo layout of the park that brought Bud and Mr. Geist, the park's owner, together but it evolved into a new title for Bud, Rockaway's Playland publicist.

Bud knew many of the right newspaper people; he had a vivid imagination combined with a great sense of humor and of course he was a great photographer.

He and the son of Mr. Geist, Dick, formulated a series of events that would ultimately make Rockaway's Playland a household name. Included in their schemes were a series of contest, some staged events designed only for the camera. They would use "models" who did not demand a wage or an agent. These photo ops were just another normal Clarity day for Rosanne and me.

One photo session that was especially memorable was the pie-eating contest without the use of a knife or fork. The "contestants" included Rosanne and me, our three Stillwaggon cousins, and Curly, who should have had an agent by then, he was called on so frequently. There were many pies, all blueberry, probably because the blueberries would photograph with good contrast and produce the best mess. On cue, we would push our faces into a pie, pretending that we were competing for the most consumed pies. The youngest cousin, Eileen, was cheating. She was feeding one of her pies to Curley, who thought he died and went to doggy heaven.

The proof of the success of this shoot was to be found in the centerfold of the following morning's issue of the *Daily News* with a generous mention of Rockaway's Playland. The models were paid in passes to all the rides while Curly was ignored.

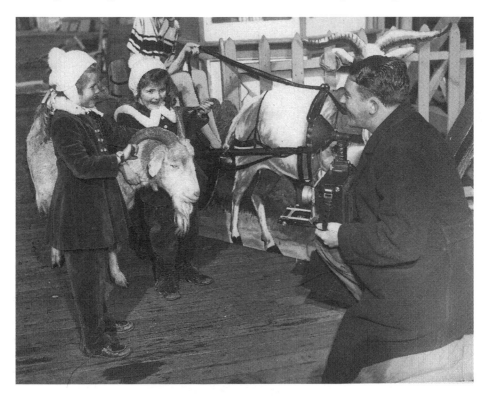

Playland added another attraction to the park and they had four legs and sharp horns. Goats found their way to Playland and, hitched to a child-size cart, they became a popular ride in the park. Rosanne and I were the only models used, or rather abused, for this one. We were dressed as cowgirls, complete with ropes and toy guns, and we were sent to location, the goats' barn. Bud directed us to stand with our backs to the goats as though I was preparing to throw the lasso. Dick was handling the two goats and he was having such a very hard time controlling his silly, loud laughter. I suspected that my father and Dick had plans for these goats that they were not sharing with Rosanne or me. They were hoping for a surprise butt attack; however, fortunately for us, the goats had no intention of cooperating. Bud managed to get a slightly different angle and evidence of this "rodeo" appeared in the *New York Daily News*.

Dick and my father were enjoying their new joint venture and became very good friends. It was not hard to enjoy Dick's company. He was a large man, tall with a big frame, a quick smile, and a hearty laugh. He had thick dark hair and wore large eyeglasses with dark rims and I am not sure why but he always reminded me of a very large teddy bear. Dick was younger than Bud, single, and loved children and we were recipients of his enthusiasm until he married and had his own family. I remember the night his first daughter was born, Dick was so excited, he called my father at one o'clock on Christmas morning to share his good news, but until then we rode the roller coaster with him. He loved the coaster and rode it with the enthusiasm of a teenager, laughing as he took us for the ride of our life and before we had time to catch our breath, he would order the operator to take us up again. He was the best advertisement for his own amusement park.

He would then walk us through the park, and with his best VIP treatment, take toys off the shelves of concession stands, handing them to us until we could not carry any more.

He became an important part of our young lives; he was the friend who played the role of a benevolent uncle. He gave us wonderful toys for Christmas and lent my brother, Michael, an elaborate set of Lionel trains for Christmas week and the rides in the park were available to us whenever we wanted.

A special memory of Dick Geist was all about a tiny tears doll. Rosanne and I played house for so many hours and my mother's living room began to resemble a day care center. There were dolls and carriages, blankets, baby clothes, bottles, and cribs in every downstairs room. We even invented an inept doctor whose treatment resulted in our babies remaining forever as infants. We named him Dr. Krug after the home delivery bread company; we preferred it to their competitor, Dugan. I can understand the make-believe game we played; there are times when I wish my children remained babies, for at least a little longer.

Some days we would dress the kittens in kimonos and wrap them in blankets, place them in a stroller, and push them around the house.

Dick and his fiancée, Phyllis, were coming for dinner and he asked us in his most enthusiastic voice if we would like him to bring us a tiny tears doll. We were so excited that it was difficult to respond in the affirmative: yes! It was actually painful waiting for the day to arrive and the morning of the big day we looked for all signs that day was changing into night.

The table was set, Curly was fed, and my parents dressed for dinner and finally their car pulled up in front of our house. They were here! Please try to imagine our reaction when they came into the house empty-handed. He really enjoyed this; he turned to Phyllis and, with a most shocked expression, said, "Oh, no, we forgot the dolls!" We really believed him and before we could shed some not so tiny tears ourselves, we heard him say, "But

I think there is something in the car. I'll have a look." Of course it was the tiny tears dolls, with so many accessories that the box was too large to hold.

We loved those dolls; mine sat on my bed for nearly sixty years until someone gently suggested it was time I let her go. Both of her arms had rotted and she lost an eye.

There were numerous contests throughout the season; contestants would sign up in advance and my mother and father would recruit the judges. The judges might be friends of the family, coworkers, some celebrities, or local politicians. The requirements were few: a nice appearance, a good sense of humor, and the ability to withstand some verbal abuse from the losing contestants.

The theme of the contest varied; there was a beautiful baby contest, a baby crawling race, a beautiful pet contest, a tall girl beauty contest, a Miss Rockaway's Playland, and others too numerous to mention.

The events were held on the fairway and the judges were seated at their table in front of the contestants while the loudspeaker system announced all the details of the judging to the gathering crowd. There were a few glitches over the years. Sometimes the contestants did not agree with the results of the judges and things got a little testy. I remember one contest when one young man lost control and was threatening the judges; it was understandable: his snake lost to the puppy. The judges actually had to be taken to a safe place following their decision.

The most notable event for me was the Beautiful Tall Girl contest. Several judges were selected; two were memorable — one for his height, appropriate for this competition, and the other for his celebrity.

Eddie Carmel was almost eight foot tall and was referred to as the Jewish Giant. He was an entertainer but not a celebrity; he was, at best, an attraction at carnival side shows but he did have a few small parts in the movies. He was happy to judge the contest and a friend of my father offered to pick Eddie up at his home and bring him to Broad Channel. Several people had gathered at our house for drinks prior to the contest. I don't think his driver knew who he was picking up, because he arrived to pick up Eddie in a Volkswagen Bug.

Joe Franklin, on the other hand, was a very accomplished radio and TV personality. He was said to be the first talk-show host and interviewed many of the major movie stars of his day, including Marilyn Monroe. He was also referred to as the "King of Nostalgia," hosting a television and radio show called *Memory Lane*.

He did not seem thrilled to be included in the Beautiful Tall Girl contest. I remember thinking, as he sat having drinks with the rest of the judges, *Why would such an accomplished TV personality want to do this small-town gig?* Perhaps he had heard it was expected to be a "gigantic event."

Another interesting Playland event that was not designed for a press release or to be publicized in any manner was a scheme between Bud and Dick. It was not talked about in our house, or at least in front of chatty Marguerite. So from the back seat of the car, I could only see the back of my parents. I noticed their shoulders were shaking, and I assumed that they were crying so I decided to be quiet and look out the window.

We were driving to the country; maybe he wanted to get out of town. They were listening to the news and it was reporting on a story about Rockaway's Playland and an escaped monkey. The poor thing had climbed up the roller coaster and the police and fire department were called. They responded to the scene to rescue the runaway monkey. My parents were not crying at all; they were laughing at Bud's latest publicity stunt, which turned out to be very successful. The monkey was captured unhurt and the name of Rockaway's Playland was on every news stations and news stand. I can report this chestnut some sixty years later without any recourse and I am sure that night the fire and police departments enjoyed the ruckus.

To keep it interesting, Playland was always changing rides or adding attractions. One year they updated their office space, adding a spacious dark room that Bud was free to use. If it was a no-school day, I would tag along with him to color and draw in their art department. I loved sitting at the large desk with crayons of every color that God ever created and then some. At my fingertips, sketch pads were awaiting my creativity. But I really enjoyed watching the office staff as they went about their daily routine. The girls were all pretty and were dressed nice; most were wearing high heels. A few girls talked on the phone, some typed, and some just chatted and I noticed they did not have to raise their hand for consent to talk. They seemed happy to be there and could also go to the bathroom without getting permission.

The morning became lunch time and Phyllis was taking orders for takeout. When it came to my order, she reminded me that it was Friday and it was a meatless day for me. I was six at that time and I don't know why that impressed me so much that it went directly to my library of frozen images. She was Jewish and she knew I did not eat meat on Friday and cared enough to tell me. I was very touched that she respected my religion.

Dick and Phyllis were the only Jewish people that I knew. They were special people in our lives but maybe I cannot count them as both Jewish; Dick converted to Christianity a few years later.

Chapter

44

My mother once said that she was always nice to spiders until the day one bit her.

The town of my childhood had two Christian churches and the population of this small island was entirely white and Christian. In these years, we had very little interaction with folks of any other ethnicity. When we traveled over one of the bridges, we recognized that some people were black, or Hispanic, or Oriental but since they did not live in Broad Channel, we never really had a chance to know them.

My father had an assignment to photograph several summer camps in upstate New York. The campers were inner-city children and since we were too young to be left home alone, we went along for the ride. The first stop was a girls' sleep camp and most of the campers were low-income black teenage girls. Rosanne and I were probably three and five that summer and this was the first time we met and played with girls who were not from Broad Channel. We loved those girls; it was a special afternoon: they enjoyed pampering us and we enjoyed the attention. We walked through the camp, holding hands as they showed us around. Later, they thought we might be tired and maybe we would like a nap in one of the many hammocks. Of course we were too excited to nap; we were having a wonderful day. We never forgot those girls; they were very special.

St. Virgilius had a visiting nurse who would visit our school maybe once a month. She had a tiny office where she looked busy but I never could figure out what her actual duties were. She was black and middle-aged and her uniform was a navy blue suit.

She was not an attractive woman; her jaw protruded quite a bit and she probably was a candidate for orthognathic surgery. The words emitting the long distance from her throat to her mouth resembled a large dragon spitting fire. She was abusive as she spoke, telling me in a pejorative tone to sit on a chair next to her, and with the heat of her fire emitting at me, I immediately knew she did not like me. At the age of seven, I had not yet met anyone who did not like me and I found her behavior both surprising and upsetting.

I was nervous, I wasn't sure why I was there, and when I began to speak, it was necessary to clear my throat, which annoyed her. She snapped at me, "What is wrong with your throat?" Things only got worse.

Every school night before we went up to bed, my mother would set three heads of hair: a brunette, a blonde, and a redhead. There was very little success with my hair; she tried to coax a few curls into my long blond hair but usually by mid-morning my curls went straight and a little wild. The nurse, in her strongest fire, asked me what was wrong with my hair: why was it so messy?

Maybe, if she had to walk the ten blocks in a Broad Channel wind to and from school, her hair would be a bit messy, but then maybe it could have been the Tincture of Green shampoo my mother used on our hair. She would buy it in O'Sullivan's, Broad Channel's pharmacy. You could not find it on a shelf; probably it was kept in a back room. I don't think they use it on humans any longer but it is possible it has been used on birds that are victims of an oil spill.

The time I spent with the nurse was a life lesson; not everyone we meet, regardless of color, will always be our friend.

Chapter

45

M y grandfather built a vacation house in the early '40s on two acres of land in Monroe, New York. There were secret rumors that he had come into money but I was never aware of where it came from, probably because it was a secret. He built it for my grandmother; it was not very large but it was a lovely field stone house. Grandma Theresa designed the plans for the house, which included using the stones from around the property. They were selected and gathered by a hired hand with his horse and wagon.

Entering the house, you would find yourself in a very lovely and spacious living room. A large field stone fireplace was on the principal wall and my grandfather often bragged that it was the largest fireplace in Orange County. The first thing you saw, however, when you entered her house was a wide, natural wood staircase that rose from the side of the living room across the second floor to form a balcony.

Grandma Theresa would have had a great time decorating this house. She placed several couches around the fireplace, anchored with large overstuffed armchairs. A favorite piece was the chandelier that hung over the center of the living room. It was an old wagon wheel with electric light bulbs that were designed to look like candles.

I assume that all of the furniture came from second-hand stores but when they were placed throughout the house, it made for a cozy, beautiful home, where the children could put their feet up or adults could lay their head down.

Each of her three children had their own small bedroom, with two beds covering most of the floor space. Grandma Theresa had her larger bedroom off the living room and occasionally I was able to sleep with her in her special bedroom. There was a sign on the mantle that read "Deer Haven"; it was Grandma's hope for the property. The ambiance throughout her home reflected all the charm of the lovely country retreat that is was.

With the exception of seaweed, Broad Channel had very little green, few trees, and less grass, and it was heaven for us kids to play and run free through the soft green fields that were brimming with wild flowers. These were special days when the family was together.

Memories are a valuable legacy and the memories we have of Monroe made us wealthy adults.

I had always thought of my grandmothers as sober, God-fearing ladies but the camera doesn't lie. An eight-by-ten black-and-white photograph taken in the living room of the Monroe house tells the rest of the story. The adults were having a party. Both my grandmothers wore large vases balanced precariously on their heads as they had abandoned themselves to the music. They were not the only ones having a rowdy time; the room was filled with the familiar faces of my family, who came very close to making fools of themselves.

My personal memories are more serene. I remember the smell and sounds of crackling wood burning in the large stone fireplace, the laughter of the adults playing badminton on the lawn, and the walks to "magic waters" to catch crayfish in the stream. It was lazy summer days with my father in the hammock and us little girls washing our dolls in basins on the lawn. I remember the smell of the cedar walls, the very cold water that ran from the pipes, and the colder water in the shower since there was no hot water heater. I remember the aroma of perking coffee and waking up to the voices of my grandparents in the kitchen.

I have special memories of my cousins Nancy and Eileen; they were the family babies and, twenty years later, I was bringing my own babies to the same house. We swam in the lake and the bravest swung from a rope into the frigid swimming hole. There was a legend that the swimming hole had no bottom and that there were uranium mines in the caves around it. There is the special memory of my election to president of the Apple Tree Fort, although some might argue it was a dictatorship.

Chapter

46

I woke up on my seventh birthday hardly able to comprehend how old I was. I was now in the second grade. My teacher was Sister Catherine Michael and this year I would make my first communion. Sister was young and maybe in another life she would be considered pretty but she could holler and yell with the best of them, although she was always very nice to me.

The nuns prepared us for First Communion with the Baltimore Catechism, rehearsals in church, and warning us to fast the morning we would receive. My mother did everything to impress upon me that this was a special day and dressed me in a beautiful white First Communion dress, long veil, new white shoes, and a prayer book I treasured.

Family celebrations always took place at home, with my mother taking care of the entire preparations, which included all the cooking. Sometime in the middle of the afternoon, the rooms began to swell with family and friends and many small children. She enjoyed a crowded house, a great party, and there were many times our house had standing room only. She loved her home and hosting a party, never complaining about the work or the mess that was cleaned up after everyone left.

I never knew until years later that she was pregnant that day. I am sure my mother never used the word "pregnant" until I was a teenager and that was with a subliminal warning.

She was in her fifth month when she delivered my sister, Michele. We were sent to my grandmother's house and we sensed that there was something amiss. There were so many phone calls and much whispering but Rosanne and I had no idea what was the center of so much interest. Two little girls who loved babies had no idea my mother had given birth. I know now that my mother had two previous miscarriages and a caring mother did not want to have to disappoint us. Bud brought us out to stay with my aunt Tootsie and, before we left, he told us about our new sister. I remember that morning so clearly: I was sitting up in bed and as he was getting ready for work, he held up his palm to demonstrate just how tiny she was. The baby weighed one pound and lived for only two days. It had to be incredibly difficult for our mother. She was in the maternity ward with new mothers who had the joy of spending their days feeding and loving their newborns until they said goodbye, leaving for home with a healthy baby. My mother came home alone, talking very little about the baby to us; perhaps it was too painful for her. I often wondered if Michele was baptized, although now I am sure she was, and where was she buried. No one ever referred to her again. My days of innocence were almost over; I had experienced a new emotion of sadness.

Chapter

47

I have some early hazy memories of when I was as young as three years old and our visits to Thompkins. I certainly do remember the commode. This was the time before there was a toilet and when a bowl and pitcher filled with very cold water was our sink.

I do have one very clear memory of a day some few years later. It was one of those wonderful, crisp October mornings. Rosanne and I jumped out of bed very early and knelt by the small, narrow windows that looked out over the enticing vista visible from the front of the house. The rectangular windows sat close to the floor and did not offer a view unless you were a seven-year-old kneeling on the floor. The windows were unique to the Greek revival design and framed with stained glass of ruby red. The Greek revival architect was often seen in the Catskill Mountain houses.

We were observing the weather, glancing to see if it was a morning for jackets and boots, but then we were visiting a farm, where it is always a morning for boots. We had arrived the night before and maybe we were really looking for reassurance that nothing had changed since our last visit. As I looked out the small window that particular morning, I had an epiphany, at that moment I left my heart in the Catskills. I saw so much beauty from that window on the beautiful autumn morning; I knew I would always find myself returning there.

It is October and the leaves have turned to brilliant shades of gold and crimson. There is a layer of dew upon each leaf and, bathed in the rays of the sun, the trees appear to be draped in crystal. Shifting our gaze to the right, we stretch our necks to see the pond. The still water is shrouded by a cover of mist that lingers after the cool night temperatures of autumn. Two white geese move regally across the water, presenting an aura of serenity and peace. This is only an illusion; these large birds are actually beastly creatures, and they will chase and torment little children.

We dress quickly, donning our barn clothes and boots, and run quickly down the stairs, hoping to pass the pond while the geese are enjoying their morning swim. Rosanne sticks her tongue at them as we run as fast as we can toward the barn.

It is early morning; the grass is very wet but the sun is burning through the mist as we reach the barn, congratulating ourselves that we arrived without incident. Running through the muddy yard, we say a "good morning" to a few dry cows, who are observing our joyful entrance, probably thinking, *City kids*.

There are two doors to the barn, the larger one for the cows and the smaller door that opens to the narrow passage that is used for graining the cows. We choose the smaller door and that brings us face to face with a row of not very contented cows. They are hungry and maybe we can help but right now we just say our hellos and give each face a rub and a pet. If we were chilly when we entered the barn, we have warmed up thanks to the heat generated by these twenty-three cows standing together in the small barn. The familiar smell of manure doesn't offend us; it reminds us that we are once again back in the country. Beneath the cows, several kittens have gathered around the udders, scouting for any milk that might have missed the pail. If they are lucky, Buster, the hired hand, will squirt some milk in their direction but not every kitten will be his target.

Eventually, Buster will give his okay to grain the cows. We take a pail and we head for the grain bin. Lifting the cover, I have to reach down almost to the very bottom to scoop up the grain. In this inverted position, a cow reaches out and begins to chew on my hair. It is an honest mistake; my hair is the color of fresh-cut hay. As I free myself from a very short and instant haircut, Rosanne is laughing very hard, maybe too hard.

We won't visit the pigs this morning but we do pass the chicken coop. The chickens are very funny. As passive as the hefty cows may be, these scrawny birds never stop complaining, protesting, and shuffling around their pen. When a girl from the kitchen arrives to gather the eggs, she lets me help and we bring them back to the kitchen, the catch of the day.

We have always been comfortable in the old house. It was spacious and clean and if the decorating was lacking Martha Stewart's style, it gave to us the happiest memories.

In many ways it was a learning experience for us to visit a home so culturally different than ours. Rosanne and I had no idea what we should do with the breakfast egg cups that sat on the dining room table. We had never seen one before. I thought it was a juice glass that you can turn over when you wanted a refill. We were introduced to the old wood stove that heated the kitchen and cooked the food at the same time. I would watch from the doorway as the girls would lift a cover from the top of the stove with a special handle and slide a few logs into the belly of the oven. The old black stove was the hub of the kitchen; at mealtime, all the activity centered around it. It was also the first time I saw the waters of Niagara Falls moving on an illuminated lamp shade. I learned very quickly to avoid the circumference of the dreaded outhouse. Eventually a full bath was added to this charming house.

We woke to the crowing of the rooster and would lie in bed for a time, listening to the sounds that told us that morning had broken and another day has begun. A door opening, a few voices from the kitchen and we were soon searching for our boots and dressed for the barn.

I don't know why we were so happy to be on the farm; there was no television or toys except for maybe a doll we brought from home. My mother would warn us not to bother the women in the kitchen and if the living room was open to children, I'll never know. The meals were not child-friendly; I was not a big fan of tomatoes, and lettuce, and potatoes, all brought in straight from the garden. I ate peanut butter and jelly at almost every meal but she did make some very good desserts.

But we did love those horses and cows. We were diligent in our participation in both the morning and evening milking. Sometimes we would just braid the cows' tails, hold a few kittens, or pet a new calf. When the evening milking was over, we would pick up our walking stick and stroll with Buster, moving the cows to their evening meadow. We walked down a country road edged with an assortment of wild flowers and a dog or two at our side. This was Buster's shining moment. He would strut proudly before the boarders, his clothes revealing his work that day and his macho cigarette hanging from his mouth. He enjoyed parading his herd and silently bragging how he was in total command. Some days we would be surprised with a new calf. We would fuss over her and Buster would delight us by naming her after one of us.

You can never appreciate just how huge and fast a work horse is unless you are a seven-year-old with a bucket of blackberries and one of these equine giants is intent on chasing you down. Rosanne and I were picking berries from the same field where the horses were grazing and we obviously caught their attention. They walked toward us and we walked faster; they walked even faster and we ran and then I felt the ground shake under me. I was not going to let go of that bucket; blackberries are not easy to pick—there were so many thorns and even more flies. Violet's grandson, who was about our age, kept calling, "They won't hurt you" but we felt it was prudent not to believe him and kept running until we reached the barbed wire fence and in one quick movement slid under the wire, dropping most of the berries.

It is almost time for breakfast; I hear the women talking in the kitchen and I can smell the aromas of fresh coffee and sizzling bacon. Soon the dinner bell will ring and we will file into the dining room, wishing everyone a good morning and finding a seat. My reaction to the dinner bell is similar to Pavlov's dogs, queuing up for food that I am not even fond of.

I don't like eggs, even if they are brown, were laid that morning, and were brought over from the henhouse straight to the skillet. In fact, I don't like eggs of any color. Pancakes would make me happy but not bacon or warm milk from the barn.

We sit outside, waiting patiently for the bell to ring, and I make eye contact with one of the geese approaching from across the road. I hurry to take a seat in one of the old worn rockers that lined the front porch, joining my parents and the other guests. We arrive as a diverse group of strangers but after sharing meals at a single table, we are now a family, if only for just for a few days. We sit together on the porch and I am entertained as I listen to stories the adults share. They talk of their life, the lack of rain, and how they will spend their day. When it is the dinner meal we wait for, Grandma and Bud will bring a Manhattan down from their room and soon they are animated and entertaining a receptive audience.

My parents were very fond of an elderly couple from Manhattan, the Dietzes. They have no children but they seem childlike in their reliance on each other. They were both soft-spoken and maybe a little eccentric but then, to us, anyone who did not have roots in Broad Channel was a candidate for eccentricity.

Mrs. Dietz was an artist and her medium was watercolors. As she walked along a country road, she seemed to step out of one of her lovely paintings. She was petite, dwarfed by a large hat, and fortified by a walking stick fashioned by a fallen branch. If Pete was not up to a walk that day, Ring, Violet's border collie, would take his place at her side. She was careful with her wardrobe and always wore full makeup, keeping her appearance easy on Pete's eyes.

Pete was a very quiet man; he moved slow and spoke low. He and Bud enjoyed the company of each other; the front porch chats had developed into a mutual friendship. They both enjoyed photography but that was the extent of their similarities. I doubt that Pete would ever lean outside an airplane for the love of the art and he probably never would toil as a longshoreman. But he was a gentleman and a talented photographer and we enjoyed his annual slide shows in Violet's dining room. Sometimes it is easy to be around a quiet man; they tend to listen.

The family time spent at the farm embossed into our spirits the things that would be valuable to us for the rest of our life. We learned to love the simple but extraordinary gifts that life would offer us: a ride on the top of a wagon of fresh-cut hay on a sunny August afternoon or the simple joy of a brisk fall day, walking on an amazing carpet of red and gold, a swim in the cold water of Red Falls, a bumpy ride with my sisters, brother, and several dogs in the back of a pickup , the summer night sky bejeweled with brilliant stars, and the thrill of swinging on a rope across the hay barn with my siblings and new friends.

Over the years, a pleasant friendship grew between our families. We enjoyed Violet's grandchildren and found her own children both colorful and very interesting. One year when we were visiting Violet's house, my mother miscarried and Violet took charge, nursing my mother as a caring, sympathetic, and loving friend. My mother never forgot her kindness.

Our week would not be complete without a ride on the back of one of those huge work horses. As we were clinging for dear life to his neck, mane, nose, mouth, or ears, Buster would walk us a few feet up and down the road. Smiling for the camera, no one suspected I was actually relieved to be back on solid ground. Minutes later, after hugs and kisses, we were pulling away to the ringing of Violet's dinner bell bidding us a safe trip, with many arms hanging out the window, waving goodbye until next time.

Chapter

48

Joseph Dunninger was a very successful and highly paid mind-reading act, although he said he was not a mind reader but a thought reader. He began his career in clubs around the country and on the radio in the mid-1940s. He worked without an assistant, which was unique to that act, and dared anyone to prove otherwise, with a reward of ten thousand dollars if they were successful. No one ever received the reward because he did in fact work alone.

It would seem that no one, including the Duke of Windsor, Babe Ruth, Jack Dempsey, or Harry Truman, could prevent Dunninger from reading their mind.

In the '50s and '60s, he had his own very popular television show and throughout these appearances, he disclaimed any supernatural powers but with no explanation for what they had just witnessed. An illustration of his art involved the US postmaster general in New York City. On live TV he asked the postmaster to reach into a conveyor belt holding thousands of letters and choose just one. Dunninger took a few minutes to concentrate and wrote what he believed was the correct address on a large piece of paper. Yes, it was the same address the postmaster read out to the audience.

Bud was invited to participate in a presentation on his live television show. He was very excited at the opportunity but was also very adamant that he would not be involved in any act that was not absolutely truthful.

Ed Clarity, Dunninger would explain to the audience with his superior stage presence, fortified with a bogus Oxford accent, which he apparently picked up in his boyhood neighborhood, the Lower East Side, would allow his thoughts to be read in a segment that involved a Polaroid camera.

Bud was instructed to go out alone into the city using a Polaroid camera, choose a subject to photograph, and return to the studio. The audience would watch in awe as Dunninger described the image on the Polaroid picture.

Bud traveled by foot around the city, executing serpentine maneuvers that even James Bond would envy. When he was confident that he was not being followed, he descended into the bowels of the city, riding the subway to a destination that remained ambiguous until he was ready to choose his target. He walked past a hotel, only to return, and, upon entering, began his search for the subject of Dunninger's gifted talent. A framed print of Blue Boy hanging on the wall of a meeting room was his choice and he quickly returned to the studio. In front of a live audience and television cameras, Dunninger read his thoughts and conjured the correct image of the Polaroid picture.

It had to be a very long journey for Bud, returning to the studio. The Polaroid camera was not used for news photography and although he would have been a fool not to familiarize himself with it, he probably broke out in a cold sweat awaiting the results. Film photography might have been diagnosed as the cause of press photographers' stomach ulcers. Imagine Bud standing in front of a studio audience and TV cameras and, with a silent drum roll, and finally the push of a button, the picture exits the camera and it is blank, but I then I guess Dunninger would have known that.

Chapter

49

The year is 1951 and I expect to meet my nemesis in September, Sister Daniel Marie. She is the third-grade teacher of St. Virgilius School and was expecting me and twenty-nine other students two days after Labor Day. Her reputation put fear in the stomach of every second grader, many who preferred not to be promoted and just remain in the second grade indefinitely. A few of my classmates were put on medication to quiet their stomachs.

She was a large woman, masculine in her height and frame, with a loud, piercing voice that shook the windows if she was annoyed. It was rumored that when she was angry, her voice had the potential to break the convent dishes.

Those who would control the fate of our future would add heat to a cold war and the fear of a nuclear holocaust continued to dominate the news and mood of our lives. Air raid sirens were installed in every town; people were building bunkers and storing water and food. Mandatory air raid drills were held in the schools of every state.

Perhaps it was assumed that teachers would take the time to instruct their students that this was a drill, only a rehearsal. Maybe they would begin by saying, "We will take a few minutes to follow instructions and with prayers for peace that we would never have to face the real thing." This did not transpire; we functioned in the shadow of fear and the unknown.

For many years, I resented Sister for not preparing third graders for those drills appropriately and questioned why she stood there and did not comfort or reassure us that we had nothing to fear. It was years later that it dawned on me that she was most likely as ignorant as we were about the drills and probably she was also very frightened.

The air raid siren sat on a telephone pole that was probably less than four hundred feet, as the crow flies, from our classroom; it was incredibly loud and amazingly close.

The noise was terrifying; it was so loud it would echo for a lifetime within my ears. I prayed it would stop; I only knew it was a signal that we were in imminent terrible danger. This was the day I walked through the gates of my paradise and my innocence and security would be lost, never to be found again.

When the blast of noise from the sirens began, we dropped to the floor and curled up under our desk. In this position, I knew this small wood shelter that doubled as my desk would not protect me from even the smallest object dropping from the sky.

I remember one boy who was probably eight years old, a little rough around the edges, and presented a street smart veneer to a class that was a bit immature. I heard his voice crying out from a few rows across the room, "I want to go home." Sister shouted back, her voice quivering with fear and at even higher decibels, "Do you want to get hit with a bomb?" Children cried for their mothers but I was too numb to speak. Mercifully it stopped after three minutes but it was those three minutes that changed my personality for life. My mind would always taunt me with worrisome, anxious, or frightened thoughts throughout the years, regardless of how carefree I might appear.

It was early autumn and we were staying at Violet's house during an Atlantic hurricane that went astray, blowing strong winds accompanied by lightning and thunder over the Catskills. I left my bed to seek shelter on the staircase; I seem to use a staircase as my place of choice to worry. My mother found me sitting there and seemed surprised that I was frightened. I think her nerves were stabilized by a hurricane party that was going on downstairs, hosted by her and Bud for the other guests. She assured me we were safe, noting that this house had been withstanding storms for over one hundred years. The next morning as we drove to town, I saw the remains of another one-hundred-year-old house that had been hit by lightning during last night's storm. The only evidence that a house once stood there was a large, black, smoking chimney and that was the beginning of my thunderstorm anxiety.

I was seven years old for the first half of the third grade and being allowed to walk home alone only meant not walking with Mary or Michael but with my classmates. St. Virgilius had no lunch room and in lieu of a gym class, we all walked home for lunch but the Claritys walked a little further than most. The conversation between the older boys this year was joking and talking all about the bomb. I sensed they were also frightened but had to put on an eighth-grade pseudo courage in an attempt to be cool, but naturally their conversations only increased my fears.

The government's plan for the air raid sirens was now a part of our daily routine. The vessel that delivered so much fear and anxiety hung directly over our heads on a telephone pole as we walked home for lunch. At exactly twelve noon, I would walk under the same excruciating noise that we were programmed to associate with fear and danger.

Dick Geist stood in our living room one summer day and he was very frightened. He was speaking in a loud voice with rapid words for several minutes without stopping for a breath of air. He was expressing his concern for the country from a nuclear attack. He spoke of churches and schools being primary targets and cities being eradicated and populations wiped out until finally I saw my mother making strange facial signals to him and I realized she was trying to quiet him but I had heard enough. I had been sitting on the couch when he came in, close enough to hear and confirm everything I suspected was true.

If the minds of this generation of children were not subjected to enough, it was followed by the next chapter and that was the distribution of dog tags. Our names and other data were printed on a metal military plate attached to a chain designed to hang around our neck. There was talk in the school yard that these tags were to identify our remains after a nuclear attack. I wondered who would be left to take care of the recording.

My mother tried to calm my fears but I knew she was also frightened and there was actually a panic among many adults. She spoke once of us leaving the city by boat if it was necessary. This almost came to fruition during the 1962 Cuban missile crisis, a very dire time for the country and the rest of the world.

Chapter

50

I continued to have a happy childhood in spite of my anxiety but there were times I would retreat to the winding stairs that led to my bedroom. If Bud was not home from work as scheduled, I was sure something awful happened to him. I would hide on the staircase and say a prayer that he was safe and would soon be home.

There was, however, another side to me. I did very well in school, could be adventurous, athletic, spontaneous, and sometimes even fearless

Well, maybe not really fearless, but Rosanne and I would pretend we were fearless cowgirls, climbing the rocks outside our house in search of outlaws with our trusted dog Curly by our side. We dressed the part, complete with guns and hats and fringed vests.

We now had a place to play other than in the narrow street; our yard was extended with fill and rocks and separated our house from the marsh, giving us a generous yard.

Cowboys were the current trendy entertainment heroes and Roy Rogers was our favorite. He starred in popular Western movies and he had his own weekly television program with Dale

Evans and Trigger. We would never miss his Sunday night show and Rosanne had a huge crush on Roy.

If it was a nuisance posing for Bud, it did have its perks. Bud had many contacts, including publicity men at Madison Square Garden, and we could visit the Garden as frequently as Ricky Nelson. We loved the Ice Capades, the circus, and the rodeo, and this year the rodeo was coming to town with Roy Rogers and Dale Evans headlining.

No matter how many times we went to Madison Square Garden, I would never get over the thrill of leaving the concourse and entering the arena. To my mind, it was as if I were standing on the side of a tall mountain, looking down into a deep canyon. The canyon today is filled with hundreds of excited children sitting patiently in every available seat. They are waiting anxiously for the show to begin. The music finally starts, the lights go up, and the arena is suddenly filled with glamorous men and women riding beautiful horses. The rodeo was always a favorite to us city slickers who rarely get to see a beautiful lady riding on the back of a great white horse as effortlessly as though she was riding the carousel.

It was arranged that Rosanne and I should meet Roy Rogers, the King of the Cowboys. We followed Bud down the long dark backstage halls of the Garden and out of a very drab ordinary door he appeared, very much like the star he was. He was in his most wonderful cowboy attire, topped off with a large white cowboy hat. He had those attractive squinty blue eyes and that sweet but macho wonderful smile. He talked to us while Bud did his thing and ended the visit with a kiss on Rosanne's cheek!

We returned to our seats to watch the show and after the finale, we joined the other children at the rail. Dale and Roy would ride around the arena, shaking hands with every hand that reached out to them. When Roy saw us, he smiled and said, "Hey, I know you." My mother was very impressed with his manners and his memory. She probably also agreed with Rosanne that Roy was very cute!

Publicity was a lifeline for celebrities in the days before any celebrity was fodder for magazines such as the *Enquirer* and *The Star*. When actors appeared in a television program, they were acting out a part; they were not the subject of these programs. There were several "movie magazines" in the '50s with beautiful photographs and controlled accounts of the lives of the movie stars and each issue would canonize a favorite personalities.

Early one Florida morning, I was preparing for a walk and as I passed the television, I glanced at the screen and saw my father. It was a surreal moment; my father had been dead twenty-four years. *The NBC Today* show was covering the recent death of Elizabeth Taylor. It included a newsreel of her meeting the press as she deplaned at Idlewild Airport. As she descended the stairs, Bud was the first member of the press she saw. It was the usual crushing crowd of press reporters and photographers that Elizabeth had come to expect.

Bud was not as impressed with the celebrities he covered as he was concerned with the success of his work. Kim Novak was very irritated with Bud when he asked her repeatedly how to spell her name; he probably had never heard of her and he was infamous for his terrible spelling. I was thirteen when Bud met Elvis Presley. Elvis was rehearsing for that famous appearance on the *Ed Sullivan Show* and Bud brought home a trophy autograph for Rosanne and me.

He was very impressed with Mohammed Ali. They met on a flight and, after chatting for a while, Bud mentioned to him that he was now retired. Mohammed answered my father, "I guess maybe I am too." I had an interesting collection of autographs thanks to Bud; it was fun but today I don't know where most of them are, with the exception of the one from Elvis.

I have photographs of President Kennedy taken at the army-navy football game, Jimmy Durante clowning with Bud nose to nose, and of course Elvis, who did impress my father with his manners. There is a photo of Bud singing with gusto with Ed Sullivan, Kate Smith, and a few others at a press photographers' ball.

Thanks to the power of the press, Grandma and Bud were treated as celebrities whenever they traveled. If they were sailing east to Europe or south to the Caribbean, they were seated at the captain's table. If they were flying, more often than not, upon entering the terminal, they were escorted to a first-class

VIP lounge and upgraded to a first-class seat before being pre-boarded. One particular vacation began the moment they shared a VIP lounge with Elizabeth Taylor. She was a very gracious lady and looked through my mother's very extensive brag book but then what choice did she have? She was a captive audience. One of my mother's favorite celebrity experiences was attending the wedding reception for Patricia Kennedy and Peter Lawford. She was not exactly on the guest list, but the press was permitted to bring their wives to the reception after the formalities. She was so very excited at the thought of mixing with the Kennedys. She returned home from the reception with a heart-shaped white satin box with the bride and groom's initials scripted in it.

When I was thirteen, I experienced my first commercial flight. Rosanne, Grandma, and I flew out to Los Angeles to meet with Bud, who was covering the Democratic nominating convention for president. The handsome young Senator Kennedy from Massachusetts was attracting a lot of press and attention.

The jet engine was not yet a component of commercial travel and our trip to Los Angeles was so lengthy that we might have missed a birthday. Our flight included two stops for refueling and we had just a few minutes to leave the plane and run across the terminal to purchase a very boring box dinner to take back on board. However, when you are thirteen, time doesn't matter when you have the opportunity to experience a new and exciting adventure.

We stayed with my mother's friends in West Hollywood. Grandma and Mildred had gone to Hollywood High together and they remained best friends through letters and phone calls. One night Rosanne and I, with the blessing of our mother and the encouragement of our host, had plans to see a movie. We walked the long and boring distance down to the bus stop on our way to Hollywood. To make it interesting, we were doing a balancing act, walking the curb, when one of us fell off and all the approaching cars abruptly stopped. We were on to something and for the rest of our time in California, we tested the traffic law.

From the window on the bus, we saw the eclectic city of Los Angeles. We were headed for Hollywood, where young, beautiful women walked in the direction of Schwab's to sit at the counter waiting to be discovered. There was also the tired and aging, still hopeful for their big break, walking the sidewalks in outlandish outfits, hoping to catch the attention of the agent who would change their life. It was thrilling to visit a city so different than ours.

Our destination was Grumman's Chinese Theater and we arrived late for the movie, so we passed the time looking at the signatures of the stars written in the cement sidewalk as we waited for the next showing. When we tired of names and handprints, we sat patiently on a bench talking to strangers who enjoyed our accent, although we would deny having one. Finally, we bought our ticket and spent the next two hours watching *The Apartment* starring Jack Lemon and Shirley McLaine.

We began the trek back to Mildred's house. We first waited for the bus and then the long walk up the hills and eventually arrived back at the house. What a loud commotion! There was so much yelling in that house, I had trouble understanding what they were saying. I did catch that they were sure we were kidnapped by the Mexicans. Maybe they should have thought of that before they sent two young girls out for a trip to Hollywood. We could have been discovered sitting in front of Grumman's. Would have served them right.

The convention was over; Senator Kennedy was both the new candidate and heartthrob. Bud was happy with his photographs and managed to get Grandma a ticket to get into the convention. We all returned to New York happy for the experience in the great state of California.

Chapter

51

It is 1951 and I am now a student in the fourth-grade class of Sr. Catherine Michael. If you have been paying attention, you know that she was our second-grade teacher and, lucky for her, we are a repeat performance. I continued to do well in grade school, mostly high nineties and frequently hundreds. I am not letting you know this to brag, but I never really came across as a student. My uncontrollable blond hair and the beginning of a slightly nonconformist personality, that was subconsciously planning to launch guerilla warfare against a boy from the block, Dennis, was not the uniform of a good student. I would always love books, had a short-lived interest in stamp collecting, and enjoyed my friends on the block and my new friends at school.

Rosanne and I had a keen interest in Michael's "junk draw." On a dull day, he would rummage through his top drawer, where he kept things that he just did not know how to throw out. So he would summon us to his room and began distributing his junk. There were some collectibles like his Boy Scout toaster designed to use over a campfire. I never did get to go camping. But all in all, one person's trash is just another sister's treasures but we were easily entertained.

I believe this might be the year that we became proficient in the design and the construction of forts. Each spring, we would collect the marsh grass cut down by the frozen bay of the previous winter and place it in the shape of our foundation. We had various designs but my favorite was a round structure with chicken wire on the top to form a roof; it resembled the grass huts you might see in the photographs of Kenya. We would find some flooring and furniture and this would be my parents' view until someone gave into their temptation to destroy it.

This year's fort was destroyed by the father of Dennis. He was the new kid on the block, a little nerdy, and maybe he tried to take on our fort or maybe we were just not nice to him. I don't remember but what I do remember is the tall, thin man with glasses and a mustache, madly swinging the long, golden grass in every direction. I don't think my mother was really very upset to see it destroyed, although she did have a few things to say to him.

The forts served as our clubhouse. Another clubhouse was a large wooden cabin boat that floated in and was wedged in between the rocks, probably the victim of a hurricane. It was a lovely fort with a large cabin. You may ask what you do with a clubhouse. We would read comic books, discuss the bomb, or just had a picnic. Once I sat for an hour writing a poem about after I died, which caused my mother to laugh pretty hard, which was rather cruel since it was not meant to be funny. Occasionally we said the rosary. Boys and girls, we were good kids, but maybe not to Dennis.

I don't remember what caused me to lock Charles and the other Charles on the block in the pigeon coop but maybe the crush had finally run its course.

Chapter

52

Bud's photographs continued to impress the city and attract attention. He was known by the mayor and the governor and our local politicians; they knew him as Ed. It has been said that the press and politicians make strange bedfellows.

Bud had a hundred stories to tell and when he did tell one I would listen closely with one ear. When I was older, I found myself always speaking about him to anyone who wanted to hear about his career, thinking he had the greatest job in the world. He was a witness to the life of the city as he traveled in interesting company, but not all those whom he photographed were people you would invite home for dinner.

An infamous member of the mob had died and was being waked in a crowded funeral home, attended by most of his coworkers. Bud entered the room, stood before the casket, and discreetly took out his camera, which was concealed under his coat, and in a split second took his shot (with his camera, not the other kind of shot). Immediately, two huge friends of the departed took Bud by the arms and escorted him out the door, a little more forceful than he would have preferred, but Bud's photo of the deceased was on the front page of the *Daily News* the next morning.

Bud was always the larger-than-life figure in my life. He was bold and daring when it was necessary and funny and entertaining in a small group or a large crowd. He was completely immersed in photography and perhaps that is why he excelled at it but sometimes it would seem as though it took precedence over what was going on in our lives.

In retrospect, when I look back, he was similar to the fathers of every one of my friends. Fathers of my childhood were the sole breadwinner and mothers stayed at home, managing the scout and school calendar, the birthday parties, the homework, and all the to-dos that accompanied parenting.

My father's responsibility was to feign a great thrill when my mother told him that for the first time I had swum across the canal or to gaze at my report card of straight A's and make a great fuss. Maybe a C would have gotten his attention. I don't remember any commotion when I won the running race but then I did come in second.

It is not that he did not give us a happy childhood; he certainly did. We knew he loved us, he was a good provider, and worked very hard around the house to keep it the way my mother loved it. We looked forward to large family picnics with the cousins at Glen Cove, and the noisy birthday parties held in our house. My mother always bought excessive birthday and Christmas gifts for us and Bud never questioned what she spent. We had wonderful holidays, with all the cousins coming for a supper that had followed dinner. There were the trips to Tompkins and Monroe several times a year and we had wonderful summer days on his day off at the beach or on the boat. We continued to celebrate the Fourth of July at my grandmother and Pop's house on their back deck. But there were no more sinking boats.

I don't remember him ever reading me a book but I do remember that he never said a word when my friend Judy got carsick and vomited all over his very brand-new DeSoto. He never raised his voice or a hand to us and I never heard any four-letter words or toilet jokes in our home. I was twelve when a friend used the sh** word and I had no idea what it meant. He never told us to clean up our plate or go up to bed; sometimes his behavior was more like an older brother than a father.

Maybe it was his Irish background—his father was as stern and cold as Bud was warm and kind—but he learned to love maybe from a little distance. When he traveled to Europe with a stop in France, he sent his three daughters the most beautiful dolls from Paris. He took the time to pick out the dolls and ship them but on the same trip he mailed me a post card from Switzerland and signed it "Bud," not "love Bud" or "I miss you," just "Bud."

As I child, I never felt a distance; he was Bud, our father, who loved us. It was as an adult looking back over the memories, but then realizing that his generation of dads evolved into fathers who are very much involved in parenting, cooking dinner, doing homework, chauffeuring their children to afterschool events... and then really maybe less is more.

Chapter

53

The birthplace of the miracle labeled education was the cramped classrooms of St. Virgilius. Only a small number of Broad Channel children attended the public school and they were the only minority of the island. Very few of us went to kindergarten; there were no teachers' aides, monitors, or computers in our classrooms. One teacher, sometimes an elderly nun, would be the sole educator for thirty-something first graders and the cost of our education was one dollar a month per family.

Most of us pre-*Sesame Street* first graders came to school not knowing how to write our name nor did we know our letters or numbers; that was left to our teacher and I think my mother researched this before she gave me the name of Marguerite.

The nuns of the Franciscan order whom we disliked, loathed, or loved were committed to filling our minds with the fundamentals of Catholicism. Their guidance produced good citizens who loved God, obeyed the law, were committed to a marriage, and lived by most of the rules of the Church and the state. For the most part, these were the people I knew growing up in Broad Channel.

Within the five hours of the school day, Sister would teach us to read and write, and study history, geography, and arithmetic. After school, Sr. Estelle would give piano lessons on a very old piano that sat in a hallway and she produced a worthy recital at the end of the school year. Before a standing-room-only crowd in the parish hall, I did a fairly good rendition of "The Sidewalks of New York." But it was the end of my music calling when Sr. Estelle left our school. I am not sure if she had health issues but she was missed. We never had a gym class or recess and we had no after-school activities.

The sisters worked without any visual aids or computers but they did have the respect of our parents. When I was a young mother, I read a column by Erma Bombeck and she wrote how we, the parents, feared the nuns and she realized the reason was that we were afraid they would give the kids back to us. The respect and cooperation from the parents made it possible for our teachers to teach and the respect for the sisters was inherent in their students.

I am sure there were many students who carried a reputation that every September would bring dread to our teachers, and also some families that were not cooperative, but there were also teachers that gave the student body anxiety and trepidation when thinking of returning to school after the summer recess.

We did have one eccentric sister and that would be our sixth-grade teacher. She was probably living with emotional problems and in today's world it might be said that her students were, to some degree, physiologically abused. Anyone who has gone through Catholic school would have a story to tell of a particular nun who believed in corporal punishment and I remember a few who had no problem using a ruler and it had nothing to do with measurements. One first-grade teacher, who subbed for as long as two months when Sr. Estelle was ill, rearranged the classroom, seating the best students in the first row and the slowest in the last seat. If you were late for school or talked out of turn, your seat was moved down the aisle to sit with a child who was socially and hygienically challenged. He was punished every time someone misbehaved.

Sister John Marie was a no-nonsense teacher. She taught seventh grade and could handle those preteen boys and girls very well. But she also had a great personality and loved to play ball in the school yard with the boys during lunch hour. She was known for having a great pitch and enthusiasm for the game. Sr. Antoinette Marie, my fifth-grade teacher, was as round as she was tall. She screamed until her face turned an unusual shade of red but she also had a sense of humor and a great smile. It was her nephew, Fr. Pius, who officiated at our wedding.

It is difficult to describe our sixth-grade teacher but one word might be used and that would be "disturbing." She never smiled, expressed humor or gratitude, or interacted with any of her students. The only thing in our favor was that she was consistent; there were no surprises. She was a competent teacher but not a good role model.

Several times a day she would have us close our books and she would speak to us with very graphic descriptions about the tortures suffered by Christians. Her introduction would be something like this; if a Russian soldier walked into this classroom right now, he would shoot me first. After months of addressing the subject with different torment, she encouraged the class to contribute some of their own thoughts. Usually what she heard was exactly what she had discussed in the class; it had been stored away in our young minds. She was the only teacher I was ever uncomfortable to be around. She never laughed or smiled and yet she was generous with her grades; my average that year was about ninety-nine. She did seem to enjoy the Christmas season; our classroom was over the top with decorations. But what surprised me most was she planned a class trip in June to mark the end of the school year. She was very brave; she took us to a Broad Channel beach.

The manmade beach was located at the end of Noel Road and was a byproduct of the Eighth Avenue subway extension. It was a cement trestle that carried the trains across the bay and to reach the beach, you had to walk with your head down under the trestle to clear the four-foot upper limit. Each day the clearing was determined by the height of the tides. If you were ignorant of the tide schedule, your retrun might find you sitting on the beach for a longer visit than you had previously planned.

Most of the folks of Broad Channel were excellent swimmers but were well aware of the danger of the strong currents that these waters carried, especially at a change of tide. However, passengers on the A train on their way to Rockaway would look down on the bay and plan to return to the Broad Channel beach for a family outing. There were no signs to warn visitors of the danger and every summer there was at least one tragic drowning victim from this tranquil seashore. Although we were not permitted to swim that day, it was a risky choice for a class outing.

She was a sad and lonely figure standing there on the beach that day, a sober contrast to the girls and boys who were thoroughly enjoying themselves. Her habit, dark and heavy and exacerbated by the heat of the June sun, dragged in the deep sand as she walked. She looked out at her charges and except for only what was essential, she never exchanged any words. I think of her often and wonder why she brought us to the beach that day. There had never been a class outing to the beach before. Did she have special memories of a visit to the seashore from her childhood? Was it a place to calm her anxieties and, as a member of her order, she could never visit the beach by herself? I wondered if she ever experienced happiness or joy or did she have some tragedy in her previous life? Maybe if we were older and wiser we would have tried to reach and know her and maybe we would have seen her smile.

The sisters lived together in a chilly convent and were sustained on a sparse and bland diet. Their day began at five-thirty in order to prepare for Mass followed by a small breakfast before going into the classroom. Their quality of life depended on the mother superior, who was also the principal of the school. One particular principal, Sister Eloise, made life hell for anyone she came in contact with. I wish I could go back and thank some of my teachers and let them know they were appreciated.

St. Virgilius School   5   1954

Chapter

54

Sometimes I have this dream. I am in the arms of a young, handsome sailor, who carries me up the gangplank and places me gently on the deck of a large ship. I then realize that it is not a dream; it is another of those frozen images waiting to thaw.

The ship is the battleship *USS Missouri*, sometimes known as *Big Mo*. She was a war hero, serving in the South Pacific during World War II, Korea, and the Gulf War. The surrender of Japan, known as the armistice, was signed on her deck in September of 1945 with General Douglas McArthur representing the United States.

In 1950, under the command of Rear Admiral Kirkland, battle commander, *The Missouri* visited New York City, accompanied by eight destroyers.

Bud, as a member of the *Daily News* staff, was invited to visit the ship and spent several days taking photographs for a feature story. Admiral Kirkland invited Bud to ride with him in his helicopter, giving him a great opportunity for a special view of the ships.

Never one to worry about pushing the envelope, Bud asked the admiral if the ships could perform some maneuvers and the admiral, over the helicopter radios, ordered some formation changes. The photographs were amazing; I am sure both Bud and the admiral were very pleased.

As he was preparing to say goodbye to the admiral and *Big Mo*, Bud was invited to the ship, this time with the family. We arrived at the ship and I looked up at that massive gray steel hero of our country (the ship, not the admiral) and wasn't quite sure how I would get up the steep gangplank with dignity and a functioning heart.

Before I had a moment to worry about it, a young sailor scooped me up in his arms and effortlessly delivered me to the deck of the ship. The admiral was very gracious and I clearly remember him standing in his cabin, taking some cash out of his pocket for us to buy ice cream.

Chapter

55

If you were in a Catholic school classroom and Sister posed the question "what is the most important day in the Catholic Church calendar year?" all hands would shoot up and one student with a smirk and confidence would answer, "Christmas." Sister would let us know that she was wrong; it is Easter. Well, I know many of us would argue with that; Easter Sunday was a nice holiday but could not compare to Christmas.

Easter Sunday meant new spring clothes; the Clarity sisters would each have a new spring coat to coordinate with the new dress, white gloves, and a new pair of black patent leather shoes. I don't know if Michael had new clothes or if he cared.

A long narrow table that stood in the living room was decorated for Easter, with potted tulips, some ceramic chickens, and six assorted Easter baskets; two were antiques from my parents' childhood. On Easter morning all six baskets were filled with mouth-watering candy. The favorite, of course, was the tall chocolate bunny with the sugar candy eyes and a pink bow around the neck.

My addiction to chocolate begins early with depravation followed by excess, and the Easter season was the infancy of my addiction. The bunny, which was missing his ears before breakfast, was just a memory by night fall.

Besides the Easter candy, we always had a few gifts, maybe a pocketbook to match the new shoes. One year we each received two live turtles with flowers painted on their shells. That day brought our total number of domestic pets to eleven. There was one mother cat, many kittens, one dog, one bird, and turtles. My mother should have been canonized or institutionalized.

This was another cousin day; my mother would set the table with a supper for the entire extended family, never complaining about the work load.

Easter week meant Aunt Mary was coming for a visit in a few days and I was hoping that Sr. James Eugene would accompany her. We loved Sr. James Eugene; she had a wonderful natural laugh and she became a good friend to our family.

On this Easter visit, we had just finished lunch and she had her arm around me and asked me how I was doing. I was at that in-between age and when I answered her, "Okay, I guess. I am too old for dolls and too young for boys," she threw her head back and laughed so hard—not at me but for me.

But it was true; I was too old for dolls and not ready for boys. I was also too old to be fighting with our neighbors. I am sure my mother was very tired of them knocking on our door but then she never was receptive to their complaints. When once the very annoying man complained to my mother that I called him a grouch, my mother just looked him in the eye and answered him, "Well, really, aren't you?" He was. I was done with forts and cowboys and Indians and I was really tired of climbing fences, which is something we did only when we were bored. I did continue to enjoy playing red light-green light, but only if I was captain of the team.

I was fairly young when I was permitted to walk to the stores by myself but I was never really alone; I would always pass friends and neighbors along the way.

We were a little town with a big heart and it was hard to believe that we were actually a part of a very big city. The shops and stores were Mom-and-Pop businesses, all owned by our neighbors with the exception of a small Bohack and A&P.

I do not remember any drunken driving scandals when I was growing up. There were seven taverns on the island and most of the folks who enjoyed a beer or two were within walking distance of their favorite saloon.

Rossi's small grocery store was a quaint shop with a country ambiance. The wooden floors and the window displays were shaded by a striped awning and the mandatory cat roamed the store searching for mice. Chocolate cookies and other delicacies were displayed in a tempting marketing ploy but my father salivated over some marinated Italian red peppers. My brother would eventually grow immune to the store's temptations. He worked after school for Mr. Rossi; riding his bicycle equipped with a large basket, he made home deliveries.

Probably my favorite shop was Glass's Bakery. It was owned and run by German bakers and I have never found cookies, rolls, or pastries as delicious as what came out of their ovens. There were booths and tables for those who preferred instant gratification or others who knew they could not resist the temptation of a full bag of jelly doughnuts. I really felt I had arrived when I sat with friends in the booth, eating my buttered roll with a jelly doughnut or cruller on the side.

Our behavior at sleepovers became a little daring when I was somewhere between eleven and twelve. The coup took place when Marianne and I would walk out of the house, very late at night, and head for the bakery. We would stand at the bakery's back door, maybe a little brazen, knocking very loudly, letting them know we were there for cookies. The bakers appeared a bit strange, probably because they spoke just a little English and possibly thinking it might be a holdup. Maybe they assumed if they cooperated, no one would get hurt because they did let us in and we purchased the cookies just out of the oven. We became their occasional midnight customers for many years, sometimes bringing with us other conspirators. We always giggled on the way home about how we thought they were going to put us in the ovens.

If you were in need of a gift or just wanted a new blouse, you could visit Ripples, a dry goods store. It had a limited selection but it was convenient, especially with the unreliable bus schedule to take us to Rockaway. Their daughter Claire changed her name to Claire Ripel during the time of her short career with the June Taylor dancers.

There were two butcher shops in Broad Channel; each had the floor covered with saw dust and I could never figure out what was the need for saw dust in a civilized town. I don't think any of the customers found it odd; they shuffled through the sawdust to reach the counter and ordered their meat. I learned later that sawdust dates back to the time when a butcher would hold up a side of beef and blood dripped on the floor; the sawdust would make it easier to clean up the mess. When my mother went to the butcher shops in the late 1940s, she would order only enough meat for a few days. Her refrigerator, a luxury after years of using an ice box, had a very small freezer, just big enough to make ice cubes for two Manhattans.

Two barber shops competed for the business of cutting men's hair and I often accompanied my father for his haircuts at Phil's, and we had one small beauty salon. I think that the majority of her cliental had to be seniors in for their monthly perm. When I passed the shop with my friends on the way to school, the strong odor of ammonia seeped out of it. We would hold our noses to repel the odor until someone gave the all clear.

A small A&P had opened in Broad Channel in 1932 with a new and unique way to shop, self-service, and there were also two delicatessens in town with the best homemade German potato salad. We were fortunate to have a tailor and Mr. Minnie, who repaired shoes.

For the most part, the island was self-sufficient and that was a lovely way to live. When our dog chased the cat through the front screen door, my father went out to buy some screening. He did not have to drive a six-lane highway to a store that resembled a warehouse and walk a half mile to find a cashier. He went to the local hardware store. In the early '50s, there was never a problem parking on Cross Bay Blvd. He would stop by Gus Coldberg's hardware store. Gus would greet my father with, "Hi, Ed, that was some photo of yours in yesterday's newspaper." After they caught up on local news, Bud had his screening, and returned home in less than twenty minutes.

When my mother was nervous and feeling stressed, she visited Dr. Werner, our family doctor. There was no prescription drug for Valium; he gave her the following advice: "Marge, every night, one half hour before dinner time, you make yourself a Manhattan." It seemed to work and she followed his advice religiously and without complaint.

We had our own local characters. Mr. Yatta was a life insurance salesman. He was short and walked with a slightly hunched back. He was a familiar sight as he would meander the boulevard daily, dressed in a proper dress suit, dress shirt, and tie, and always the impressive briefcase. Occasionally, he was mistaken for a Jehovah Witness. Grandma Theresa found him quite unnerving. She felt that his "good morning" was "more of a question than a greeting," suspect that he might be making a payment on a policy in the very near future.

The most notable business was the office of John McCambridge. He was a local boy, a war hero, and when he came home from battle, he married Margaret and gained a large, lovely Broad Channel family. He opened a real estate office and he was a broker for several forms of insurance. He also offered a service for collecting the ground rents due to the city. Many innocent folks went to Johnny for insurance or mortgage advice; he was an important citizen in our town, similar to a mayor but without any authority.

His office space was divided into two rooms; the front room was occupied by his assistant and at first glance it reminded me of a scene from *Great Expectations* by Charles Dickens. I saw Miss Havisham sitting at the desk and although she did not wear the white of a bride, she reigned in a space of an organized chaos and excessive chain smoking. The entire office was a controlled mess: file folders piled high on the desk, chairs, or across the floor. An ash tray that had probably sat on the desk for weeks was overflowing with cigarette butts, tattooed with her lipstick of the darkest red. Later it became apparent that the cigarettes that overflowed in the ashtray were her afternoon smokes; the morning remains had been thrown in the trash pail.

Mr. McCambridge's respectful life as a broker, a friend, and a neighbor came to a sad standstill when his other life was exposed; John had a very serious gambling problem and he gambled with the payments his neighbors and friends entrusted with him.

Life insurance and car insurance payments were not made. Mortgages were in arrears and the scandal swept through the island as only gossip can, but this was not gossip. These were payments made by the poor and middle-class hardworking people who trusted John with an important part of their life.

There was a couple who splurged on a new luxury car and after a few weeks, the car was stolen. She reported it to the police first and then John and all he told her was, "I will call you back." He did and his only comment was, "Joan, we have a problem." It was only the tip of the iceberg that was beginning to surface.

I have finally reached my favorite destination, O'Sullivan's pharmacy; it was both the cultural and civic center of Broad Channel. There were four separate entities to this store. The first unit was the newspaper and magazines, cigar, cigarette, and candy section.

I would spend the little spare change that I might have in this part of the store. I loved movie magazines and the other magazine that printed the words to all the current songs.

I loved to imitate Annette Funacello or Connie Francis but I had such a terrible voice, so I sang the rock and roll lyrics very loudly but very far from the possibility of any one's hearing me.

As a freshman in Stella Maris, I tried out for the glee club, auditioning for the music director, the nun who would decide my fate. After two painful lines, if she did not approve of what she heard, she would wave her arm, her sleeve swinging to the music and in one continuous motion, signaling us failures out of the auditorium without even a sympathetic invitation to try again next year. I never did; I don't have to be told twice.

In her defense, years later, I was in our kitchen when I heard this dreadful noise coming from the living room. I told Dad, "I don't know what that terrible sound is in there but you better get your gun and put it out of its misery." A few minutes later, we realized it was my recorded voice on the answering machine.

I would spend some serious time making my next O'Sullivan's purchase, choosing the candy as though it might be the last candy bar I would ever eat. Long after the war ended, my mother rationed sugar, so this was a serious selection.

I stood there in deep thought for so long, I would begin to irritate Frank, but if you shopped in O'Sullivan's as a child, you knew that children could irritate Frank with very little effort. Some years later, I thought Frank had mellowed as he smiled a lot more and that then I realized that it was not Frank who had changed; it was me.

There was a small area in the back of the store that served as a US post office. It was convenient but it was also intimidating. Mrs. Brust was the official postal clerk and she took her position very seriously as she stood behind the caged window. If I had a package to mail, my knees would go weak as I approached her through the bars. She would examine the package and, with the same detached lack of sympathy as the glee club moderator, hand the package back to me with a smirk and tell me it was not acceptable. I witnessed the early stages of post office employees behaving postal and to this day I have some anxiety that my packages will not meet the standards of the US post office.

If you had impetigo, poison ivy, strep throat, syphilis, or any communicable disease, it would never be a secret. There was one pharmacy in Broad Channel and all of your prescriptions went through your neighbors, Bill and Frank and Mrs. O'Sullivan, who worked behind the counter. In wasn't until the mid-'60s that the birth control pill was available and women who chose to use it would drive to the next town, where there were several drug stores. Bill was a quiet, nice man and was very helpful, offering his advice whenever he could without overstepping his professional boundaries. There were exceptions, however; when Mary gave birth to Donna, she went in to buy a few dozen pacifiers and Bill warned her against using them. Mary was so angry, she left the store swinging her arm with the car keys in her hand and, of course, the car keys flew out of her hand and went straight down the sewer.

Now we get to the best part of the store: the old-fashioned soda fountain. I believe a fountain such as this was the birth place of the egg cream and the beginning of many romances.

We would climb up on the swiveling stools and order an ice cream cone or soda.

Malted milks were popular and they served the best hot chocolate made with milk and topped off with real whipped cream. They carried loose-packed Breyer's ice cream and the soda jerk would reach down into the large containers and scoop out your favorite flavor; mine was chocolate chip.

After dinner, the corner was a meeting place for the teenagers and before I came of age, still wedged in my preteen years, I would walk up to O'Sullivan's to get the early edition of the *Daily News* for Bud. He was anxious to see if his photograph was on the front page. I didn't mind; I enjoyed watching the older kids and tried to blend into the crowd but never with success, so when the truck pulled in and swung the papers from its rear out onto the curb, I purchased the *News* and walked home.

Chapter

56

Bud's work took him to many interesting locations, and if they were local, Rosanne and I would go along. We had some enjoyable experiences; one I remember very well was the International Toy Fair held in New York City. It was an opportunity for toy manufacturers to present their new product line to the wholesale buyers. Bud was covering it for the *News* and a toy fair sounded to us like a tolerable invitation. The toys were amazing. Some would not be available to the public for some time; these were the toys of the future.

Mayor Impelletteri and his wife, the first lady of the city, were present, along with some other local politicians, to support the event. The mayor's wife seemed bored or lonesome as she stood alone, holding her mink stole and a gift of an orchid corsage. Determined to overcome my shyness, I did my civic duty and made an effort to talk with her and provide some entertainment. She did respond; she asked me to hold her mink while she visited the ladies' room. When she returned, I assumed she was grateful; she gave me the orchid corsage. Rosanne and I returned home that day with new roller skates and an assortment of other new toys. All in all, it was a good day.

Another interesting occasion was a weekend trip to Greenport, a beautiful scenic town on the North Fork of Long Island. We tagged along with my parents but really we had no other choice since we were too young to stay home. Bud was covering a story on the oyster beds off Long Island. We stayed at a large old hotel that reminds me of the hotel from the movie *The Shining*. It was the Booth House, an old and historical hotel, and I found it both beautiful and scary. Climbing the old wide staircase, I kept my eyes on the door to each room, not knowing what was lurking behind.

The next morning we visited a plant that farmed the oysters. It was a bright, sunny day as we boarded the boat that would take us out to the oyster beds. The captain explained to us how the oysters are moved from the bed to different bed every seven years, to help preserve the beds.

He was very hospitable and when we returned to his office, he went to his desk. He must have been very important; he had a very large desk. He removed a box that held about a dozen pearls. There was one very large pearl; it was probably twice the size of the others. He opened up his hand and invited me to choose a pearl to take home. Yes, I took the largest one; I think I was set up.

Years later, the Booth House was destroyed by fire and the oyster business in Greenport, Long Island, was over; the beds had been over-fished.

Chapter

57

Bud's career seemed like a dream but there was an overwhelming stress that accompanied the glamor. The *Daily News* logo read "New York's Picture Newspaper" and that it was, but it had strong competition. There were many rival newspapers in the 1950s: *The Mirror, The Journal American, The New York Times, The Post*, and the *Herald Tribune*.

When a high-profile story broke and a photographer was sent out to cover it, he had better not only get the shot that tells the story but the pressure was on to get the best shot.

I overheard Bud talking at a party about the time he missed an important shot and he told his editor that the film dropped out of his hand and rolled down the sewer. I guess he felt that claiming clumsiness was better than admitting that he failed to return with the picture for the story he was sent to cover.

I always loved looking at Bud's photographs; they were funny, beautiful, and always told a story. Later on when I began to take an interest in photography, he was my most important critic and encouraging fan.

Occasionally Bud would be assigned to cover the airport since air views were either the only possibility or the best approach for certain photo opportunities. The *News* had two small planes based at a Long Island airport and he worked with a very capable pilot, Al Dibelo.

There were days when it was very quiet and maybe even boring but it was not boring on the day of July 25, 1956.

The headline of the *New York Times* the following day read: "THE ANDREA DORIA AND STOCKHOLM COLLIDE, 1,134 PASSENDGERS ABANDON ITALIAN SHIP IN FOG AT SEA; ALL SAVED, MANY INJURED."

The *Andrea Doria* was a beautiful ocean liner and it was said to be the safest ship sailing the oceans. The hull had eleven water-tight compartments and any two could fill with water without endangering the safety of the ship. It also had a double bottom, running the entire length of the ship, a design for greater stability in the event of a collision.

There were many prominent passengers aboard that night and all their luggage was packed in preparation for their arrival in New York at 9:30 AM the following morning. That night, at 10:30 PM, after the final dinner of their voyage, probably most passengers were heading to their cabins, anticipating an early morning wake-up call.

At 11:22 PM, the *Andrea Doria* and the Swedish ship, the *Stockholm*, collided in thick fog and passengers of the *Andrea Doria* were ordered to abandon ship.

The Italian ship was listing so severely that the crew was able to launch only two of her lifeboats and an urgent call went out for help through the *Stockholm*, since the *Andria Doria* had very little power and was not able to use her radio to keep in touch with other ships.

A French ship, the *Ile de France*, was the largest rescue ship but a freighter, the *Cape Ann*, was the first to arrive and was able to get in between the two damaged ships, taking the first survivors on her eight life boats. Her radio message at 3:55 AM was that it would be suicidal for a search by plane because the fog was so thick. Flares were sent up to identify the sinking ship.

There were many critically injured passengers and forty-six of these succumbed to their injuries.

I try to imagine the tragic view as seen from the cockpit of the plane. There were two *Daily News* planes hovering above the wreckage, each photographer anxious to get the dramatic shot of the Italian ship as it sank. The fog had finally lifted as they looked down on the chaos as ships and boats raced to the scene, all converging around the two damaged ships. The Coast Guard of course was a first responder after the *Cape Ann* and the *Ile de France*. Many smaller fishing boats and private cruisers rallied around the damaged ships, looking for survivors around the two large ships. One ship had a crushed bow and the other was listing so severely that it was only a matter of time before it went under.

At the same time Bud was hovering over the rescue mission, the seventh floor of the *Daily News* building on Forty-Second Street in Manhattan was experiencing a different chaotic scene. The seventh floor was the home base of the editorial staff and picture desk. It is an open, immense room, noisy with the clacking of typewriters and telephones. The air is foul from the cigarettes burning at almost every desk. This particular day, they are writing about the *Andrea Doria* and my father's immediate boss, George Schmitt, was doing his crazy dance, sweating and stressing and I'm sure cursing that one of them had better come back to the paper with a front-page shot. But there was a problem, a problem that he might not yet have been aware of: both planes were running out of gas.

At the scene, both pilots talked to each other by radio, trying to decide who would go back to Nantucket to refuel and who would stay behind, but the ship was taking her time before making her final bow and neither man had that option or their front-page shot.

Bud had taken many excellent photographs of both the *Stockholm* and the *Andrea Doria*. His photograph of the *Andrea Doria* shows her listing, not yet ready to say "ciao," and I'm sure it made the front page. When they returned from Nantucket and flew over the scene for a final circle, all that remained were the bubbles coming up from her final resting place.

One man, Harry Trask, a Boston newspaper photographer, convinced a pilot to take him out to the scene and he agreed but only on the condition that they fly over the ships and keep going, returning immediately. He did get the sought-after shot and won a Pulitzer Prize.

The *Stockholm* was repaired at the cost of $1 million and sailed under the name of *MS Athena*, and the *Andrea Doria* would remain a beautiful but sad legend. Over the years, many books have been written about the *Andrea Doria* and she attracted the challenge of several scuba divers. The first dive was successful; the wreck was found and pictures were published in *Time* magazine but diving conditions were very dangerous and sixteen scuba divers died while exploring the wreck.

Chapter

58

It is 1956; the seventh grade and the class of '57 is almost there. There is definite change in the air. I noticed it when I approached a few girl friends in the school yard and it seems they have made a group decision not to talk to me. My picture had been in the newspaper and I assumed it offended them. I never spoke about the photos, it meant nothing to me, but we have entered the moody years and nothing is predictable. That afternoon, seven of my good friends have arrived almost at my front door; one of the girls wanted her book and I guess she thought she needed reinforcements. Bullying is not new.

It was over before it began, but there were some of the winds of war blowing through my own head. It was a difficult age for both my mother and myself. I was angry all the time at her; it was probably hormonal but I felt isolated from her and the rest of the family.

Mary and Danny were dating and it was pretty obvious that it was serious. They were happy and they were fun to be with. My mother enjoyed having an adult couple at the table. I would agree it had to be more fun than a sulking twelve-year-old. Michael was out to sea with the merchant marines and I think my mother was in need of adult conversation and was also looking forward to the empty teenage nest. On every occasion our table was full of couples except for me: my mom and Bud, Grandma and Pop, Mary and Danny. Rosanne and I had separate friends now, so I lost her to her best friends, Patty Anne or Bobby. But it was more than that; my mother did not seem to have much interest in what I was thinking. She was ready to move forward, beginning with Italy or France.

RMS. 'FRANCONIA'. West Indies Cruise. 1966

She was planning her first trip to Italy and she was so excited and I was happy for her. She had so many things to take care of but no one was taking care of us. The three sisters were on their own for two weeks and I was the cook. Thinking back, it was really pretty funny. She left cash and a menu and I followed it religiously, cooking our vegetables in her precious pressure cooker. Our meals were boring but fortified with vitamins. We knew no other way. One afternoon, Michael brought home a cadet from Kings Point, and invited him to stay for dinner. I was well-trained; I began our meal with the offer of a Manhattan.

We did have a few parties while they were away; we weren't angels. Since I was only twelve, the guests were strictly Mary's friends and some people she didn't even know. The house was very crowded and the noise could be heard a block away. There was no damage; the bikers stayed outside and the police left without any arrests. I was enjoying my rebellious spirit and I came close to making French fries for dinner.

Rosanne and I and a few of our friends from the block began the "Sunshine Club." We would meet once a month on Friday night and some called it a boy-girl party. When someone's parents would not allow them to attend, word reached the nuns and they were pretty angry. It was very innocent except of course for the nude prints that decorated the basement. We always sang "Let the Sunshine In, Face It with a Grin." We listened to Bill Haley and the Comets, ate potato chips, and drank orange soda.

The seventh and eighth grades brought me some new freedom. With a few friends, we rode bikes on the boulevard and took the bus to the movies or the beach. When we had some babysitting money, we would take the A train to the Brooklyn stores, to buy some new clothes or the latest must-have .45 records. On a cold winter day, the boys and girls would ice skate on the canal and if the ice on the bay was adequately thick, we would walk out on the frozen water. One afternoon, my buddy Judy and I were watching her younger sister Nancy and we convinced her to test the ice on the canal before we put on our skates. Within minutes, her little sister fell through the ice and we threatened her not to say anything to her mother as we pulled her out. We spent the afternoon giving her hot chocolate and keeping her warm and praying that she would not tell.

No one enjoys graduation as much as an eighth grader. We had our leather autograph books with the tassel on the zipper and we worked the room to get everyone's signature greeting. Every page was either a very solemn prayer or a wish for success on the road of life and then there was always a very silly poem. The day after graduation, the book was placed in a drawer and packed away forever with our Girl Scout badges and old report cards. No eighth grader ever told their teacher, "Just mail me the diploma, I'm busy that day."

I was at the principal's desk one day, doing an errand for Sister, and I saw a list of candidates for general excellence and my name was one of three. At the graduation ceremony, no one was awarded the medal; they gave each one of us a medal for something generic. I received diligence; I would have preferred general excellence.

We chose our graduation dresses hoping to steal the spotlight and enjoyed the dance for us thirteen-year-olds who were trying not to act our age.

I met Marianne in the summer of my discontent, not really unhappy anymore but restless. I did not have any close pals; the girls from St. Virgilius would always be my friends but I needed someone a little more adventurous and silly.

I think Marianne and I were destined to be both friends and soul mates; we loved the same good, silly, and innocent fun. We would never tire of playing some very dumb pranks and thinking we were so very funny. Her parents both worked nights and during the summer, I spent many of those nights at her bungalow, getting very little sleep. The high tide came close to her back door and we would swim in the moonlight, pretending we were members of the synchronized aquatic swimmers of Jones Beach. We would have our walks up to the bakery at midnight for chocolate chip cookies and our favorite was the phone call pranks. *American Bandstand* was the most popular television show for teenagers and we all knew the regulars on the show and who they were dating. Dick Clark featured the top performers and we swooned to the music and wore our hair just like Justine, or at least we tried to.

We discovered one day that if you screwed off a part of the phone near the mouthpiece and when you placed a call, you would sound very far away. We called Danny Mundy, who was now married to my sister Mary, and told him we were in Philadelphia and we were going to be on *American Bandstand* in one hour, please run down the street and tell my mother. We were both yelling very loud to convince him we were in Philly and he believed us and went to see my mother. He was very excited to tell her to hurry up and put on the television. She did not blink an eye, just said, "Danny, did you really believe those two?" It was great, just the best.

Chapter

59

September 1957 would mean the beginning of my high school years and Stella Maris was my parents' school of choice. The school, a compound of many ancient buildings, sat facing the ocean. In a previous and more exciting life it was a resort hotel complete with secret passageways in hallways that led to nowhere. It was beyond repair, very expensive to heat, and the plans for a new school were ready to put into reality. I don't know if they were waiting for me to arrive to begin the project, but our freshman classes were on split sessions. We had no gym, just twenty minutes on the beach once a week, and the cafeteria was the first building to go. But we did have plenty of young construction men walking the halls and we were told in, no uncertain terms, not only not to talk to them, but not to walk anywhere near them. Naturally, most of the girls ignored the warning and wound up in detention.

As we sat in world history, local history was being made in Rockaway. The old historic buildings were wrapped in cables and as we sat in the classroom we watched as they pulled on the cables and sent the buildings to an undignified end.

There was an unfamiliar yet pleasant, earthy smell when I first entered my freshman home room and then I realized it was leather. The girls of Belle Harbor and Neponsit carried leather bags; the girls of Broad Channel and Ozone Park preferred vinyl. We were a classroom of many cultures and neighborhoods but that uniform we wore was just that: it was the great equalizer. No one would attempt to carry an air, not wearing those blue, granny, thick-heel shoes.

I made some of my closest friends in Stella; it was similar to a sorority. We were free to be our silly selves and our behavior and appearance would have been very different if boys were on board. We knew everything about each other. We were happy to learn if someone was going steady and sympathized when someone broke up with her boyfriend. When I began to model for Clairol, everyone, including Sister Monica Joe (it was really Joseph), wanted to know every last detail. I found new friends who would never replace my old friends but I did spend many weekends in Belle Harbor with Marilyn, who became a very best friend. Mary lived in Woodside and she came to Stella in her sophomore year after being expelled for high crimes from another Catholic high school. She was accused of taking a different boat home from a school trip up the Hudson. Needless to say, there was a boy somewhere in this story.

In addition to traveling to Belle Harbor, I made many trips to Woodside and gained another group of new Irish friends. Mary lived on the sixth floor of a building on Queens Blvd. On one of my visits to Woodsine, the elevator was not working, so we took the elevator of the adjoining building to the roof, crossed the roof, climbed over on to her roof, and went down one flight of stairs to the apartment. Another new experience for me. Mary's family rented a bungalow without an elevator in Rockaway for the summer and she also became a best friend.

But I always felt I was placed in the wrong school. It was Stella Maris Commercial High School. Our classes were all about typing and steno. We were being trained to be secretaries who would wear only modest dresses and accessorize with white gloves and hats. Walking down the school hall, you could hear the sound of fifty manual typewriters clicking away as the girls, resembling trained mice, were tested for speed. I could never understand why your self-worth would depend on whether you could type sixty words a minute. Some words have more letters than others. I could probably type sixty one-syllable words of three letters in a minute but, really, what would it matter in the whole scheme of things if your entire letter took fifteen or even twenty minutes to type? I would never master Pitman shorthand. I believe there was a firewall around my brain to prevent shorthand from creeping in. Just think, all that time remembering those symbols that I could never distinguish, only to find myself in an office with dictaphones. I also had no interest in a job that involved running for some grumpy man's mail and asking if he takes cream in his coffee. I would have preferred a school for photography but in 1957 that was not an option for most girls.

Chapter

60

My mother had a total trust in me and maybe that made her life easier but it was a heavy burden for a fourteen-year-old.

Marianne and I realized we needed some friends to hang around with and we had two choices: the crowd from O'Sullivan's or the other crowd at the candy store on Noel Road. Mary and Danny's friends were with O'Sullivan's, so I took a brave walk to Noel Rd.

Most of the group was a few years older than me so it took a bit of courage to attempt to break into the crowd. I would walk up at night to the corner and just hang around for an hour until, one night, when maybe she felt sorry for me, Barbara Paz asked me with her no-nonsense personality, "So you want to hang out with us?" I was thrilled.

The candy store, which actually sold very little candy, was a dark and dreary building with sloping, uneven floors that supported a soda fountain and lunch counter. A young couple, Mary and Tony Arragalli, had recently purchased the business and probably did not realize that a substantial number of teenagers went along with the title. It was a second home to most of us, our social teen center. The store sold the usual cigarettes, candy, ice cream, and all the other junk food you would ever need. But the most important fixture to most of us was the juke box. I will always remember Barbar Paz feeding the juke box with quarters and singing along with her latest favorite hit.

The guys would usually stand on the corner outside the store. I think a requisite for a successful hangout was that perfect corner. Most of them were much older than me and except for a date or two with Harold, they were friends but not boyfriends.

It was a place for me to go for those formative years beginning at fourteen. A few times, we would help out behind the counter, but I did not last long; I made the perfect vanilla egg cream but I would usually taste it to see if it was just right and then any egg creams I made were my own.

There was probably nine teenage girls in our crowd, all very different and yet very much alike. There was Mary Ellen, Eileen, Terry, and a few other girls who had a crush on Jerry, and the rest of us who did not. Maureen and Donny were going steady and she definitely did not have a crush on Jerry. Fran's house was the place to flop. We gossiped, ate junk food, and on the weekends had the occasional pajama party. Barbara Campbell and Jeanette and I remained good friends after we left the corner and then there was Joyce, whom I regret was a victim of our good-natured teasing. And I don't think she had a crush on Jerry but maybe.

We were teenagers, it was the late '50s, this was our time, and that was clear every time we dressed. You might say we were compliant rebels. On a Sunday after Mass, we divided into two teams and played handball, dressed of course in our tight pants. The candy store was our handball wall and Noel Road was the court. Jeanette was the only capable athlete. As we were hitting that ball all over the court, a police car pulled over and asked if we were a gang; it seemed very funny but I think they really just enjoyed chatting with some pretty girls. For the most part, the girls on the block all got along but there were always the volatile hormones just waiting to explode.

The guys in our crowd were just like any other guys in the '50s; they drank beer and drove their cars, not necessarily at the same time, well maybe. Cross Bay Blvd. was a drag strip on certain summer nights. A crowd would gather to watch the races and the police seemed to look the other way. A few Broad Channel boys were killed on this strip.

We had fun during those years; there were beach parties or just hanging out on the back deck of one of the waterfront bars, usually taking an unexpected swim before we went home. I was not a smoker and never took a beer or a drink. My mother never worried about me, which always amazed me. Hitchhiking was common but not for me. However, Marianne and I did highjack a car one night but we had a good reason. We had this pizza and it was getting cold. We had a long walk home so when the light turned red, we jumped into a car that had stopped for the light. The driver, a middle-aged man, was a bit startled but we paid him no mind and the only thing we said was, "Eighteenth Road and hurry." We arrived the half mile safely, politely thanked him, and disappeared into the night.

We had a few creative floats in the Labor Day parade. One year we were cave people; we all dressed in furry animal prints and we sang "Alley Oop" for as long as it takes a parade to travel two miles, but my favorite was the year of the hay ride. We wore Western costumes and rented a horse and wagon. Our float was a huge success; the horse behaved and that was fortunate because the only horsepower these city boys knew were their outboard motors. Finally the horse had enough and it was time to return him and the wagon back to Brooklyn.

I went with several of the guys to return the rig and we crossed the bridge into Howard Beach without a problem, fortunate that this was not the toll bridge. I don't know what they charge for a horse and wagon. Understandably, we were hungry when we reached New Park Pizza and we parked the horse, relieved it was not parallel parking. We did park with the skill of an Amish farmer, to the amazement of all of us. The problem occurred when we were pulling out. There was some damage to a rather lovely unoccupied car. I think the owner would have some trouble believing a witness who would report that it was a horse and wagon that hit him and it just got away.

We took Linden Blvd. but I don't remember who was driving. No one noticed until we rode two or three blocks but when we did look back, we saw that we had taken the chrome trim and bumpers off almost every parked car along the road as we rode blissfully into the sunset.

During the summer, we would walk the bridge to 110th Street and dance to the Irish music in Rockaway's Irish town. It was magical, walking the streets with the music coming at us from every corner; I was happy to be there. They were carefree days as only it can be as when you are being fifteen.

There was a girl from Rockaway; she was a bit older and more street wise than me, and was bothering me at school, naturally over a boy. One of the older girls from our crowd warned her to leave me alone but some rumors were flying that she was coming to Broad Channel.

Our guys were members of the "Nut Club" football team and it was a fall Sunday afternoon and they were playing on the home field. They were changing into their uniforms in the only place available, behind the bushes. I don't know why but someone said that some troublesome crowd from Rockaway had arrived. It was only another rumor but the entire football team came running from the bushes to the field when they heard we might need help—most of them in their underwear and shoulder pads; someone was wearing his helmet, maybe for protection. It was very endearing. They were good guys and good friends.

I remained close friends with a Barbara C. and Jeanette but most of us went our separate ways. I will never forget any of them, especially Barbara Paz, Barbara C., and Maureen, who passed away long before they should have. I loved them all.

Chapter

61

There is another line in my favorite Anny Tyler novel, *Ladder of Years*, that always comes back to me. I will paraphrase and you might enjoy it also: "She tried so hard not to be like her mother and one day she looked in the mirror and she was just like her father." There are days I am my father and other days I am my grandfather; on my best days I am just like my mother, but on most days I never have their courage.

They were of strong character, brave and resilient. They were made of the stuff it takes when you build your home in the path of a hurricane. You might wonder why, when Dad and I were married in 1963, we did not settle in Broad Channel. There was one explanation and it was a hurricane.

Hurricane Donna swept across New York State in September of 1960 and it was the only hurricane to affect every state on the East Coast. The winds tormented the coast line and gusted to one hundred and five miles per hour and the storm surge reached eleven feet. The old-timers, who called the Rockaways home, said it was the only time they remembered the ocean and the bay meeting over the Rockaway peninsula.

My father was cautious when preparing for the storm and decided to stay at home. He could photograph the storm from a front-row seat and be with Grandma to do whatever they could to protect the house. He moved the car to higher ground and secured anything around that would become a flying projectile. While they were securing and removing, I walked the few doors to sit with Mary and ride out the storm with her. She was in the ninth month of her first pregnancy and Danny was at work when weather reports were warning of a "cat-3" storm.

The two sisters watched through the window as the tide began to rise in the street, never noticing until it was too late that the water was coming in the house not from the front or back door but from underneath. It came very fast, rising high through the floors in every room. We did not know in what direction to run first. She was a month short of her first anniversary and all her furnishings were in bridal condition. We made a clumsy attempt to move things or grab something as it floated by. The tide was moving up the walls of her little house and then we noticed a small piece of luggage under the water. She had packed a bag for her baby — clothes to bring her home. That was probably the most painful moment of our day.

While we were having our own discouraging battle with nature, my father was experiencing his own confrontation, standing in high water against the house with winds pinning him against the large living room window in our house. He was holding off a very long wood cabin boat that had floated in and was capable of breaking through the wall of our living room.

I don't remember anyone panicking that day and Mary never appeared to be upset or scared. I think she has salt water running through her veins.

Her house still had phone service and when the eye of the storm had passed, she had a call from a young mother who lived a few doors up the street. They were friends and neighbors. Loretta thought she smelled smoke in her house and was frightened. She was alone except for her six-week-old baby. Mary should have never gone out or into the water but she and I walked up the street in waist-high water to see if we could help. When we reached the house, I took the infant from her arms and we headed back toward my sister's house. It was a huge responsibility for a sixteen-year-old to walk with such a tiny baby through very deep water. I was never sure where the curb was or if I was heading toward a pot hole. We weren't aware of it then but Mary had cut her foot and was bleeding. Our neighbor, John Ahlmeyer, came along dressed in hip boots and rain gear. He took the baby from my arms and walked us back to Mary's house, where the water had begun to recede. Eventually the storm passed, as most storms do; the water left her house dirty with some occasional seaweed tossed about. Danny was able to get home from work and took Mary to the hospital to have her foot stitched while I remained to scrub the walls and floors. As I was scrubbing and mopping, I thought to myself that day, *This is a difficult price to pay for the beauty of the bay*. Mary had a healthy, beautiful baby girl a few weeks later and named her Donna Marie.

Chapter

62

It is the fall of 1960 and, doing the math, I am in the autumn of my sixteenth year. I returned to Stella Maris as a junior, ready for another year. An elderly sister, who did her best teaching an inattentive class of sophomoric girls, had died during the summer. We were receiving some accusing glances as we walked through the halls to our next classroom.

Most of our crowd had left the corner but we would continue to see each other. A few girls had steady boyfriends and the rest of us were just chasing dreams. I surely had my share of dates but no one measured up and my mother began to worry.

My hair never changed, maybe a little darker, but what teenage girl doesn't want to reinvent herself? I began with Clorox for a short time before I noticed the smell would clear a room. I then tried, unsuccessfully, a few other safer products. Eventually I found my way to Clairol located in Manhattan and it was the beginning of a sixteen-year relationship. They actually liked my uncontrollable blond hair. I was hired to do their trade shows, which almost never interfered with school, and met two new best friends, Marilyn and Rosemarie. I knew I could never model clothes; I was not five-seven. However, Clairol sent me to several photographers as a hair model and for many years they would call for magazine work. Clairol was like a family to me during those years: the hairdressers, clinicians, models, and salespeople. I formed many friendships during those years and had wonderful haircuts.

Graduation came around before we knew it. I remained a dreadful typist but graduated with the coveted New York State Regents diploma. It was a bittersweet day for so many girls. We hugged and kissed and vowed to see each other again and knew we never would. Most of us would marry and have children and live happily ever after, but not all. There were deaths; three girls I went through school with committed suicide.

I met your father, tall, dark, and handsome, at an Irish town bar. It was a blind date and immediately I fell, and it wasn't just his baby-blue Buick convertible; I knew he was the one. I was very happy and so was my mother. Ted had to adjust to life in

Broad Channel; on one of our first dates, I warned him to park his car up the street on the boulevard, and then to roll up his pants and remove his shoes coming down to the very end of the street to my house that sat next to the bay. It was a moon tide. He also had a serendipitous meeting with my father. Ted knocked on the door and my father answered, "Hi, I'm Bud. Would you like a Manhattan?"

This concludes my lengthy memories... There are those who might not agree with everything I write but then they are my memories, memories of before you were born.

33855385R00172

Made in the USA
Charleston, SC
25 September 2014